The Cambridge Manuals of Science and Literature

T0352056

NEW ZEALAND

Maori carving

NEW ZEALAND

BY

The Hon. SIR ROBERT STOUT,
K.C.M.G., LL.D.

CHIEF JUSTICE, AND FORMERLY
PREMIER, OF NEW ZEALAND

AND

J. LOGAN STOUT, LL.B. (N.Z.)

BARRISTER OF THE SUPREME COURT
OF NEW ZEALAND

Cambridge:
at the University Press
1911

CAMBRIDGE UNIVERSITY PRESS
Cambridge, New York, Melbourne, Madrid, Cape Town,
Singapore, São Paulo, Delhi, Tokyo, Mexico City

Cambridge University Press
The Edinburgh Building, Cambridge CB2 8RU, UK

Published in the United States of America by Cambridge University Press, New York

www.cambridge.org
Information on this title: www.cambridge.org/9781107630406

First published 1911
First paperback edition 2011

A catalogue record for this publication is available from the British Library

ISBN 978-1-107-63040-6 Hardback

*With the exception of the coat of arms at
the foot, the design on the title page is a
reproduction of one used by the earliest known
Cambridge printer, John Siberch,* 1521

FOREWORD

MANY hundreds of books have been written on New Zealand, but none of them has attempted, in a short space, to deal with all the matters on which we have touched in this book. Our object has been to present New Zealand in her different phases to those who have not seen our Dominion. It is impossible in a small book to do more than deal briefly with our subject. We hope, however, we may have succeeded in faithfully showing in a brief way what New Zealand is, and what has been done by her people. Full information can be obtained from many larger treatises. A list of books dealing with New Zealand, and her publications, is to be found in the New Zealand Bibliography prepared by the late Dr Hocken and published by the Government.

R. S.
J. L. S.

WELLINGTON,
NEW ZEALAND, 1911.

TABLE OF CONTENTS

LIST OF ILLUSTRATIONS

CHAPTER I

SECTION I

INTRODUCTORY

THE Dominion of New Zealand comprises all territories, islands and countries lying between 162° east longitude and 173° east longitude and between 33° and 53° south latitude, and in addition the Kermadec Islands, a scattered group situated between the parallels of 29° 10′ and 31° 30′ south latitude and between the meridians of 177° 45′ and 179° west longitude, and the Cook group and other islands situated in the South Pacific Ocean within the Tropic of Capricorn and lying approximately between the meridians of 156° and 170° west longitude.

The original boundaries of the Colony of New Zealand were fixed by an Imperial statute (26 & 27 Vict. c. 23) in the year 1863. There was a prior Proclamation of Captain Hobson on the 30th January, 1840, which excluded small portions of the main islands, and a further extension by Royal Letters Patent in 1842, but the Imperial statute of 1863 first fixed the boundaries for constitutional purposes.

These boundaries include the following scattered islands and groups of islands : the Auckland Islands (50° 32′ S. and 166° 13′ E.), Campbell Island (52° 33′ 26″ S. and 169° 8′ 41″ E.), the Antipodes Islands (49° 41′ 15″ S. and 178° 43′ E.), the Bounty Islands (47° 45′ S. and 179° 0½′ E.), and the Chatham Islands lying between the parallels of 43° 30′ and 40° 20′ south latitude and the meridians of 175° 40′ and 177° 15′ west longitude. There are also several smaller islands adjacent to the coasts of the main islands of New Zealand.

The Kermadec Islands, which include Raoul or Sunday Island, Macaulay, Curtis and L'Espérance Islands, were annexed to New Zealand on the 1st day of August, 1887, by Proclamation by the Governor under authority of an Act of Parliament authorised by Letters Patent dated the 14th day of January, 1887; and the boundaries of the Colony were further extended to include the islands of the Cook group and other islands by an Imperial Order in Council dated the 13th day of May, 1901, from a date to be appointed by the Governor. The date appointed by the Governor's Proclamation was the 11th day of June, 1901. The principal islands of the Cook group are Rarotonga, with an area of 16,500 acres, its chief town, Avarua, being the seat of the Federal Government and Islands Administration, Atiu, Mitiaro, Mauke, Takutea and the Hervey Isles. The extended boundaries also include other adjacent but distinct

Mitre Peak, Milford Sound

1—2

islands, the most important being Mangaia, Aitutaki, Palmerston, Niué or Savage Island, Pukapuka or Danger Island, Rakahanga, Manihiki, Penrhyn and Suwarrow.

New Zealand proper comprises three main islands and various smaller adjacent islands. The main islands are the North, the South or Middle Island and Stewart Island. The two former contain a total area of 102,993 square miles out of the total area of 104,751 square miles of the whole Dominion. The two main islands are separated by Cook Strait, which is some 12 miles across at its narrowest part, widening out to 90 at its widest, and forming an invaluable waterway for sea-borne traffic. These three islands are as a whole hilly and, in parts, mountainous in character, but there are large areas of plain and undulating country of various degrees of productiveness that are available for pastoral and agricultural purposes. The estimated area in the North Island fit for agriculture is 13,000,000 acres, and the purely pastoral area 14,200,000 acres. In the South Island the areas are 15,000,000 acres and 13,000,000 acres respectively. The area of land in occupation in 1908–9 was returned at 38,204,349 acres. The unproductive area in the North Island is estimated at 300,000 acres and in the South at 9,000,000 acres. These areas include barren land and mountain tops unsuitable either by reason of their

Mud Volcanoes, Tukitere

altitude or the poorness of the soil for agricultural
or pastoral purposes.

The country is well watered, especially on the
western coast, and it is rarely indeed that any ill
effects are suffered on account of droughts.

In the North Island there are numerous mountain
ranges, and several isolated volcanic peaks, in varying
stages of activity.   It is in this island that the finest
thermal regions are situated, which are invaluable as
scenic attractions.   Certain of the hot springs are
effective in the treatment of rheumatism, gout and
kindred disorders, while others are effective in skin
diseases.   The Government has erected sanatoria and
bath houses at the chief centres, those at Rotorua
being especially fine.   In the centre of the island is
Lake Taupo, which is about 20 miles across either
way, and is the largest inland expanse of water in the
Dominion.   Like Lake Rotorua, and its surrounding
cluster of lakes, which lie some 40 odd miles to the
N.N.E., it has on or near its shores a thermal region
which is much frequented by tourists.   Fifty miles due
east of Lake Taupo is Waikare-Moana, which is famed
for its forest beauty.   The chief rivers in this island,
the Thames, Wairoa, Waikato, Mokau and Wanganui,
are suitable for and are used as industrial waterways.

The South Island has a chain of mountains rival-
ling the Alps in their rugged grandeur, and called the
Southern Alps, running throughout nearly the total

The Great Geyser, Wairakei

length of the island. Aorangi (the "cloud piercer"), or Mt Cook, the centre of this Alpine region, situated in the middle of the island, rears its ice-bound head to a height of 12,349 feet. All around are extensive glaciers of exceptional beauty, the greatest being the Tasman, which has a length of 18 miles and a width of over a mile, and is therefore of greater extent than the Alletsch glacier in Switzerland. Besides this Alpine region, the west coast of this island is penetrated by numerous sounds or fiords, in many places walled by precipitous mountains thousands of feet high, in others hemmed in by gentler slopes covered with virgin forest to the water's edge and having a beauty and grandeur peculiarly their own. It is in this island, inland from the Sounds, that the fine cold lake district is situated. The principal lakes are Wakatipu, Te Anau and Manapouri, and all have a distinctive beauty. The rivers of this island, the Wairau, Taieri, Mataura and Clutha (the latter the largest river in the Dominion) on the east, the Buller, Grey and Hokitika on the west, and the Waiau on the south coast are more or less navigable, though navigation on the west coast rivers extends at most a little way from their mouths. The other rivers are either rough mountain torrents or wide shingle beds, with a small volume of water except when in flood. There is also a thermal district in this island, at which there are well-equipped baths and a sanatorium.

The Geyser Valley, Wairakei

There are many fine harbours in New Zealand, the two best for commercial purposes being Waitemata Harbour and Port Nicholson. Upon the shores of the former is situated Auckland, the Queen City, the one-time capital and the largest city in the Dominion, while upon the slopes of the hills abutting on the latter stands Wellington, the present capital, whose wharfage, accommodation and shipping facilities need not fear comparison with many of the chief mercantile ports in the world.

The climate of New Zealand ranges from sub-tropical in the north to one resembling the south of England in the south. Its chief characteristics are an abundance of sunshine, a good rain supply, and a rather excessive amount of wind, without the extreme gales which rage in winter time around the coasts of Great Britain. Records of sunshine are taken at different centres, and rival those of the finest climates in Europe, an average of over 50 per cent. of the possible sunshine being recorded. At Napier, a town on the east coast of the North Island, the instrument in 1908 recorded 2692 hours 29 minutes, being 62 per cent. of the possible sunshine, or an average of 7 hours 23 minutes per day throughout the year. As will be seen from a study of an atlas, New Zealand lies in a corresponding latitude in the southern hemisphere to Spain and Italy in the northern, and its climate approaches that of Italy more nearly than that of any

Mount Cook and Hooker River, Southern Alps

other European country, with this difference, that
New Zealand having an insular climate the extremes
of temperature are not so great. The mean temperature ranges from 50° to 55° Fahrenheit, the extremes
being approximately 30° and 80° F. The annual mean
temperatures of some of the chief towns are: Auckland, 59° F.; Gisborne, 57·2° F.; Wellington, 55·25° F.;
Christchurch, 52·8° F.; Dunedin, 50·4° F.; and Hokitika, 53·25° F. The average annual rainfall for the
North Island is 51·35 in., and the corresponding figures
for the South Island are 46·63 in., while the average
number of days upon which rain falls is 151 for both
islands.

As would be expected in a country which enjoys
such an equable and temperate climate, the inhabitants are for the most part exceedingly healthy, and
the death-rate is extremely low. The average death-
rate for New Zealand has been for the last ten years
9·8 per thousand. In 1908 this rate sank to 9·57,
and further decreased to 9 in 1909. The mortality
amongst children under one year of age is only 75 to
the thousand, a rate much lower than that in the
countries of Europe.

The Dominion is rich in minerals. Gold and coal
are the most important, and are extensively worked.
There are, in addition, large deposits of iron and copper
ores, but the distance from the great manufacturing
centres of the world does not admit of their being

Lake Ada, Milford Sound

worked to advantage at the present time. Nearly
every known mineral is found in some part of the
country, though often in small quantities. The annual
value of the gold export totals over two millions
sterling, and the output of coal is about two million
tons annually. Besides its mineral deposits, New
Zealand is rich in forest lands, and many fine timbers,
amongst which may be mentioned the Kauri pine—
whose resin is exported to the value of about half a
million sterling annually, and is unrivalled in the
manufacture of high-class varnishes—are profitably
milled. There has been a great amount of wasteful
deforestation in order to make room for the growing
agricultural and pastoral population. Another in-
digenous product is New Zealand flax (*Phormium
tenax*), the fibre of which is useful as a material for
the manufacture of ropes and twines, and has gradually
come to command almost as high a price as Manilla
fibre in the world's markets.

The waters around the coast of New Zealand
abound with fish of various species. Most varieties
are edible, and compare favourably with the fish of
Great Britain. An export trade is carried on with
Australia in frozen and smoked fish. There are extensive oyster beds in Foveaux Strait, upon which
many vessels are employed dredging. In other parts
there is found a variety of rock oyster which is highly
prized. Trout are plentiful in most of the lakes,

Nikau Palms

rivers, and streams, and attract many disciples of the gentle art, but the attempts to introduce salmon have not met with any immediate success. Sportsmen can also count upon obtaining shooting of all kinds, including deer stalking, duck, quail, and pheasant shooting.

New Zealand is well served in the matter of transport. In the early days a large fleet of small sailing vessels engaged in the coasting trade. This was especially so in and around Auckland, where the numerous bays afforded safe and ample anchorage, and where many Maoris were settled who had agricultural produce for sale. Since the introduction of steam the sailing vessels have become fewer. Many of the few remaining have been fitted with auxiliary oil engines.

In 1909 coastwise steam vessels of an aggregate tonnage of over eleven millions entered and cleared the various ports of the Dominion, whilst the corresponding tonnage of sailing vessels was but slightly over a quarter of a million. In addition to this nearly one million and a half tons of oversea shipping entered and cleared in the same year.

New Zealanders are great travellers, and a fine service of local, British and foreign shipping companies supplies their wants. The foreign, intercolonial and coastal vessels are of a high standard, efficiently manned, and in several instances luxuriously appointed.

Kauri Trees, N. Auckland

In 1870 there were but 46 miles of railway constructed in the Colony, and these were in the South Island. Now, in 1910, the Dominion can boast of 2717 miles, and a passenger traffic of over ten millions, producing a revenue of over one million pounds from railway passenger fares.

The four large cities have modern electric tram services, and smaller cities are following suit. Roads are now made all over the islands, and there are only some "back blocks," as distant settlements are called, that are not easily accessible by well-formed roads.

Section II

THE PRODUCTS OF NEW ZEALAND

WHAT a nation can produce is ever a vital question. Suppose the answer were to be, "Splendid men and women," would not the nation be honoured? The Maoris were an able race, perhaps the finest native race European settlers have ever met with in any country. It is true that under aboriginal rule the land was not much developed. The fishings were small, and the cultivation not extensive, and they tended neither flocks nor herds. The vegetation of the islands showed the possibilities of production. Noble trees of various kinds and rich grasses existed

before ever white men landed on its shores. The
European settlements are not old. Wellington and
Auckland were founded in 1840, Taranaki in 1841,
Nelson in 1842, Otago in 1848 and Canterbury in
1850. Yet to-day the trade of New Zealand amounts
to over thirty-five million pounds, and she has many
flocks of fine sheep, some of which she exports for
stud purposes to sheep-rearing countries like the
Argentine; she has also notable herds of many
species of cattle. In 1909 her sheep numbered over
22,000,000, her cattle nearly 2,000,000, her pigs about
a quarter of a million, and her horses about 360,000.
This is surely a large development for 70 years or
less, and her people are not yet a million of whites.

It is in agricultural and pastoral products that she
excels, for she has not the winters of Europe and
America to contend with. Her cattle and sheep do
not require housing in the winter, and it is not in
many places that winter feed has to be provided for
them. Of late years the export of frozen meat has
led to the neglect of grain production, but if the
price of wheat and oats should again rise, a large
grain export would follow. She had in 1908–9
252,391 acres under wheat, and the average yield was
34·75 bushels per acre and the produce 8,772,790
bushels. No country can excel southern New Zealand
in oat production. The oats are heavier than Scotch
oats, and a yield of over 100 bushels per acre is not

rare. The average yield for 1909 was 46·46 bushels an acre and she had 18,906,788 bushels as her crop. The produce of the dairy has risen into prominence in recent years and she exported in 1908, 229,971 cwts. of butter and 280,798 cwts. of cheese, and in 1909–10 the value of dairy produce—butter and cheese—was nearly £3,000,000. She produces barley, peas, beans and all kinds of vegetables, and her fruit export is but yet in its infancy. Apples, pears, plums and other fruits grow in profusion, and in the North Island grapes, oranges, lemons and figs. The tropical Island territories yield fruit in abundance and that useful product of the coco-nut palm, "copra," from which is extracted the oil so useful in soap-making and other manufactures. Indigo is also largely grown and in some islands the diving for pearl-shell forms a profitable local industry.

To remedy the evils of deforestation, the Government in the thermal region and other districts is making large plantations of trees that will soon form a valuable asset. In 1908 New Zealand's trade with the United Kingdom was £23,585,617, whilst the whole of the Commonwealth of Australia, which had then more than four times the population of New Zealand, was £59,354,993. New Zealand has many industries yet in the primitive stage of their development, and it will be found that she can be the home of a large population. Her annual frozen meat export has risen to

2,500,000 cwts. and to more than £3,600,000 in value.
In 1882, the first year of this trade, she sent away but
15,244 cwts., of £19,339 in value.

For the financial year ending 31st March, 1910,
her exports were, excluding specie, £21,467,387 and
her imports £14,773,821. Her internal trade is large
and the spending power of her people greater than
that of any European country, though she has not
the wealthy classes of which old nations can boast.

Section III

PEOPLE

It is very often asked, Of what European race is
the white New Zealander? The present census returns of those not native-born New Zealanders give
a fair approximation of the birth-places of the ancestors of those born in the Dominion. Two settlements were organised under two churches, the Otago
settlement under the Free Church of Scotland, and
the Canterbury settlement under the Church of England, and the earliest settlers of these two provinces
were mainly Scotch and English respectively. In
other districts the early settlers were mainly
English. There is a religious census taken as part
of the general census, and roughly speaking the

churches show the nationality of the people. Anglicans and Methodists are mainly English, Presbyterians mainly Scotch and north of Ireland, Roman Catholics almost wholly Irish.

The last census gave the different birth-places of the people as follows : there were 68·26 per cent. of the white persons in New Zealand in 1906 born in the Dominion, 5·35 per cent. were born in other colonies of Australasia, making in all 73·61 per cent. colonial born. There were 23·53 per cent. born in the United Kingdom, namely 13·13 in England, 0·24 in Wales, 5·38 in Scotland and 4·7 in Ireland. Of the other European population the largest number come from Germany. There were 2·24 per cent. of continental European colonists, coming from Germany, Denmark, Austria-Hungary, Sweden, Norway, France, Italy, Russia and Switzerland. The percentage of religions will perhaps show the nationality better. There were 41·51 per cent. of the people Church of England, 22·96 per cent. Presbyterians, 14·32 per cent. Roman Catholics, 10·56 Methodists, 2 per cent. Baptists, 4·07 of no denomination, *i.e.* freethinkers, agnostics, and persons who have no religion, or object to state their religion. There are very few Jews, only 0·21 per cent. There is no Australian colony that has so great a proportion of people of Scotch descent. The number of marriages solemnized by their clergy will give an idea of the vigour of the different denominations.

Of marriage ceremonies performed in 1908, 26·37 per cent. were performed by Presbyterian clergy, 24·96 by Church of England, 14·58 by Methodist, 11·02 by Roman Catholic, 7·84 by clergy of other denominations, and 15·23 by registrars without any religious ceremony. The numbers attending religious service have been compiled from returns made by the churches, and they show the Presbyterians to have the highest attendance, and the Methodists the highest attendance considering their numbers. The returns show 52,103 Presbyterians, 49,496 Anglicans, 41,512 Roman Catholics and 41,428 Methodists attending on an average the weekly Sunday services. The most Scottish settlement has the most books in public libraries, namely Otago, with 126,101 books. Auckland has 121,575, Canterbury 120,501 and Wellington 99,251.

Is there any difference as yet apparent in the habits and customs of the colonists from their kin in the United Kingdom? New Zealanders who visit the birth-places of their ancestors complain that there is not the same joyousness in the homeland that there is in these islands. This can be seen, they say, on any holiday. It is suggested that the greater social freedom, the greater comfort, and the sunny skies are the cause. There are more holidays south of the line than in Northern Europe, more amusements, more sport. Wealthy classes, like those in

Britain, who spend their time in week-ends, in shooting, fishing, and in sport, are rare in New Zealand. There are few that do not have to work. But amongst the less wealthy perhaps there is more attention paid to amusements than in the old country. Considering the population there are more theatre-going people, more people who attend races and sports of various kinds, and even more golfers. The fact that many of the rivers are full of trout has made fishing also somewhat common, and shooting is indulged in by a class that would have no shooting in England.

There is an adaptability in a colonial that is often absent in his home-reared brother. A colonist is able "to turn his hand," as it is said, to anything. His occupation, especially in the earlier days, changed often. He is more resourceful, and has more initiative than one brought up in Europe, and he seems to get on better amongst Americans than the Englishman seems to be able to do.

Their resourcefulness and initiative are shown in the large number of patents applied for by young colonials in spite of the fact that the higher manufactures have not been much developed.

Utopia has however not yet been established in New Zealand. It has its social problems as well as the countries of Europe. There is much waste in the colonist's life. That can be proved by the sums spent on alcohol and tobacco, and on all kinds of sport. The absence of the thrift that existed in Scotland in the earlier half of the last century is often bemoaned by old Scottish colonists, and no doubt there is need for teaching colonists that economy is the best investment. In spite of this fact the deposits in Post Office savings banks totalled £12,159,294 in 1908 and in other savings banks £1,352,972. The total in 1909 was £13,557,806, while the deposits, excluding Government deposits, in ordinary banks at the end of the financial year of 1909 amounted to £20,386,367. The capital invested in building and investment societies is £1,588,606. In life insurance offices 127,721 policies, of the capital value of £31,447,101, were in existence in 1908, in addition to which there are 49,435 industrial life assurance policies, amounting to £1,188,920. The value of land and improvements belonging to settlers in 1909 was £271,516,022, divided amongst 143,243 freeholders.

These figures show that notwithstanding generous expenditure the million odd inhabitants, whites and Maoris, have not been especially thriftless.

CHAPTER II

In 1642 Abel Janszoon Tasman, a Dutch navigator, sailing east from Tasmania, which he had discovered and named Van Diemen's Land, after the Governor of the Dutch settlement of Batavia in Java, sighted New Zealand. He called it Staaten Land, a name which was then applied to a supposed southern continent stretching to the south of South America. The only parts of New Zealand that came under Tasman's observation were the north-west corner of the South Island and part of the west coast of the North Island. The natives, whom he called Indians, were encountered near what is called Separation Point, to the west of Golden Bay. They treacherously attacked and murdered part of Tasman's crew. The scene of this attack was called by Tasman Murderers' Bay and is now known as Massacre Bay. The hostility of the natives prevented his landing, and he continued his voyage across Blind Bay to D'Urville Island, where he watered his ship and then sailed up the west coast of the North Island, taking his final departure from Cape Maria Van Diemen on the 6th

July, 1643, about three weeks after he first sighted New Zealand.

There is no account of any other navigator visiting New Zealand until the arrival of Captain James Cook in 1769, 126 years afterwards. Recent research by Mr Robert McNab, a New Zealand historian, amongst the records of the *Bibliothèque Nationale* in Paris, has discovered the fact that by a strange coincidence, when Cook passed up the east coast in that year, a French vessel called the St Jean Baptiste, commanded by De Surville, was at anchor in a bay near Mongonui. De Surville's journal gives an interesting account of the natives, with drawings of the Maoris and their implements ; and also contains charts of the locality visited. Captain Cook had charge of an expedition whose main object was to observe the transit of Venus, but he was also directed to re-discover Staaten Land that Tasman had seen. The route he followed was round Cape Horn to the Society Islands. He made Tahiti, called by him Otaheite, his headquarters, and after having taken the necessary observations of the transit, sailed south on his voyage of discovery. Following instructions, he sailed south until he came to the fortieth parallel of south latitude, and then sailed west. On the 6th October, 1769, he sighted New Zealand, anchoring off Poverty Bay, which he so named on account of the difficulty he experienced in obtaining the necessary supplies and water for his ship. He anchored not far from the spot where the Cook monument is erected, near the present port of Gisborne. Leaving Poverty Bay, he sailed as far south as Cape Turnagain, and then coasted northward, landing at various places, and spending some time studying the country and its inhabitants. At Mercury Bay he hoisted the Union Jack, and took possession of the island on behalf of His Majesty. The North Cape was rounded on the 16th December, 1769, and after a tedious passage down the west coast, he came to anchor in Ship Cove, in Queen Charlotte Sound, which is one of the finest harbours in the north of the South Island. Here he careened his ship for cleaning and refitting purposes. During these operations which occupied some weeks, he explored the surrounding country and waters, many portions of which still bear the names he gave them. Whilst in this sound, Cook took possession of it in the name of His Majesty, and called the sound Queen Charlotte Sound in honour of the Queen. Sailing from Ship Cove, Cook passed through the strait which still bears his name, and circumnavigated the South and Stewart Islands, thinking the latter a portion of the mainland. On the 23rd March, 1770, he passed Cape Farewell, and after rounding Stephens Island he proceeded to D'Urville Island, and cast anchor within two or three miles of the place where Tasman had anchored more than a century before. He stayed here sufficient time to refit and water his ship, and then shaped his course for home, going by way of the east coast of Australia. It is not necessary to detail the events that happened in Cook's second and third voyages. In both of them he visited New Zealand, calling at Dusky Sound, which he had discovered, but not explored in his first visit, and also at Ship Cove, and gained further knowledge from his intercourse with the natives. After his last visit in 1777, New Zealand was visited by many travellers before the sovereignty of the British nation over it was officially proclaimed. In 1791 Captain George Vancouver, who had been a midshipman on board the "Resolution" during Cook's second voyage, renewed his acquaintance with Dusky Sound, calling in to refit, on his way to explore the north-west coast of America, and in 1793 Malaspina with a Spanish expedition touched at the same harbour.

The next visitors to New Zealand were the sealing gangs, which commenced their operations in the southern portions of the South and Stewart Islands, and the adjacent island groups. Sealing proved to be a profitable venture for more than twenty years, when owing to the ruthless slaughter and the absence of a close season, the seals were practically exterminated. Whalers began about the time sealing stopped, to engage in the pursuit of their industry. Whaling stations were established in the far south and around Cook's Strait, and frequent visits were made to ports and harbours in the far north. Britain, Australia and North America supplied their quotas of vessels, and New Zealand became their rendezvous in the southern seas, and the scene of many a deadly quarrel, and many wild orgies.

In the years 1808 and 1809 the Rev. Samuel Marsden approached the Church Missionary Society with a view to enlisting their support in commencing missionary work in New Zealand, and obtained as assistants from the Society two laymen, William Hall and John King. With these two enthusiasts, Marsden embarked for Australia in 1809 in the convict ship "Ann." It was on this ship that he met Ruatara, a Maori chief belonging to the Bay of Islands, who had visited England to see the King, and to gain some knowledge of the world. Marsden was able to show some kindness to Ruatara who had been shamefully treated, and this chance meeting proved most providential. Without the chief's help Marsden might never have been able to establish himself in New Zealand. On reaching Australia, it was not thought safe, owing to local disturbances, to proceed to New Zealand immediately, and it was not till 1814 that Hall and Thomas Kendal, a new arrival from England, were sent by Marsden to open negotiations with Ruatara. The chief returned with them to Sydney, and on the 19th November, 1814, Marsden, accom-

panied by Kendal, Hall and King, sailed from Sydney
Cove, and after an uneventful voyage reached the
Bay of Islands on the 22nd December, 1814. The
first Anglican service was held on the northern shores
of the Bay of Islands on Christmas Day, the 25th
December, 1814. A monument erected to Marsden's
memory marks the spot where his historic service
was held. This was the beginning of the Anglican
Mission, which afterwards had for its heads Arch-
deacon Williams, and many notable churchmen,
amongst whom was Bishop Selwyn, afterwards Bishop
of Lichfield in England. The Anglicans were not
left long without rivals in the field. The Rev. Samuel
Leigh, a Wesleyan Methodist, had visited New Zealand in 1819 while on a voyage in search of health,
and in 1820 we find him stirring up his fellow Wes-
leyans in England to undertake missionary work in
New Zealand. He was successful, and was made
superintendent of the mission. Whangaroa was fixed
upon as the site for the station, and on the 11th June,
1822, the foundation of the building was laid. The
mission was not a success : almost immediately after
its foundation troubles with the natives occurred,
and in January, 1827, the party returned to Sydney.
The Wesleyan Mission was re-established in November of the same year at Mangungu, and later further
stations were erected at Kawhia and Whangaroa.
The Roman Catholic Mission under the leadership of

Bishop Pompallier reached Hokianga on the 10th January, 1838, and finally settled at Kororareka in the Bay of Islands, establishing further establishments at Whangaroa and Mangungu. The first Presbyterian settlement was not established till March, 1848, when an expedition under Captain Cargill was sent out to Otago by an association of lay members of the Free Church of Scotland. Presbyterian church service however was held in Wellington as early as 1840.

Whilst missionary enterprise was thus beginning in New Zealand, traders were also beginning to turn their attention to testing its capabilities. It was known as suitable for the rendezvous of whalers, and the fitness of its timbers for ships' spars was known even in Europe. In 1813 certain Sydney traders unsuccessfully petitioned the Governor of New South Wales to be incorporated or chartered as a company to exploit New Zealand. Their ideas were modest. The Company was to have a capital of only 200 £50 shares and to be managed by two or more directors. Two vessels were to be procured, and there was to be a survey of the north island and trade with the natives. Factories were to be established, and the petitioners desired that their exports and imports should alike be free from customs duties.

An attempt was made in 1823 to set on foot a scheme to colonise New Zealand. Baron Charles de

Thierry communicated with Earl Bathurst, the then Secretary of State for the Colonies, asking for aid and permission to establish settlements in New Zealand. The reply given was that New Zealand was not considered a possession of the Crown. Shortly after this a Captain Stewart, after whom Stewart Island was named, was able to float a trading concern to cultivate flax and export timber from Stewart Island. The firm of Messrs T. and D. Asquith supported Captain Stewart's venture and some capital was sunk in the enterprise. The undertaking was not financially successful, and in 1827 the last vessel belonging to the Company was sold in Sydney.

In 1825 the first New Zealand Company was promoted in London, and obtained the promise of a charter from the King. This Company purchased some land from the Maoris and subsequently sent two ships to the colony, the "Rosanna" and the "Lambton." The vessels reached New Zealand in 1826. The first call was made at Port Pegasus in Stewart Island, and from there the vessels proceeded to their destination, the Thames, calling at Port Otago, Port Underwood and Port Nicholson on their way up the coast. The Thames was reached in November of the same year, but the hostile appearance of the natives so dismayed the immigrants that it was decided to return to Australia. Calls were made at the Bay of Islands and Hokianga. At

the latter place certain lands were purchased from
the natives, and a few immigrants remained. The
land obtained was not occupied, and nothing more
was done in the way of systematic colonisation for
several years, the only immigrants being a few traders
and whalers from Australia.

In 1823, owing to the disturbances amongst the
natives, and between natives and traders, the Governor
of New South Wales considered it advisable to appoint a British Resident in New Zealand. This was
done, Mr James Busby being appointed to the position. The experiment was not deemed a success by
some of the residents in New Zealand, and in 1837
led to a petition for protection being addressed by the
settlers to the King. It was during this year that
the New Zealand Association was formed. This association had for its objects the British colonisation of
New Zealand. The Government of the day was
hostile to the movement, and a Bill introduced into
the House of Commons in 1838 was defeated. Early
in 1839, however, the New Zealand Land Company,
afterwards merged into the New Zealand Company,
came into being. Its promoters contained many men
who had been connected with the Company of 1825,
and the Association of 1837, and its master mind was
Edward Gibbon Wakefield. On the 12th May, 1839,
the "Tory," the first vessel fitted out by the Company,
sailed for New Zealand. Her destination was Cook

Strait, and the port she hoped to reach was Port Hardy in D'Urville Island. The expedition was under the command of Colonel William Wakefield, and was composed of the leader and E. J. Wakefield, Charles Heaphy, Dr John Dorset, Dr E. Diffenbach, Richard Dudley, a Maori boy, and Colonel Wakefield's servant. The vessel had a crew of twenty-seven under the command of Captain Chaffers. The "Tory" made an exceptionally fast passage, and dropped anchor in Ship Cove on the 17th August. She remained in Queen Charlotte Sound until the third week in September, and then left for Port Nicholson, arriving there on the 20th September, 1839. Colonel Wakefield made large purchases of land, in and around Port Nicholson, from the natives and made what preparations he could for the expected colonists. On the 22nd January, 1840, the "Aurora" arrived with the first immigrants sent out by the Company, and the settlement of Wellington was established on the shores of Port Nicholson. The Company continued active operations for many years, and up to the year 1843 it had sent out over 9000 immigrants and founded Wellington (1840), Wanganui (1840) and Nelson (1841), and had lent active support in the colonisation of Taranaki (1841), Otago (1848) and Canterbury (1850), most of the land purchases for these settlements being arranged by its officers.

Shortly after the "Tory" left England the British

3—2

Government awoke to the necessity of establishing
its sovereignty over the islands, and despatched
Captain Hobson, R.N. to New Zealand as "Her
Majesty's consul and as eventual Lieutenant-Governor of such territory as may be ceded to Her Majesty
in the New Zealand Islands." His instructions were
to obtain recognition of British sovereignty from the
native chiefs, and to induce them to agree that no
lands should in the future "be ceded either gratui-
tously or otherwise except to the Crown of Great
Britain." Any territory acquired was to become a
dependency of the government of New South Wales,
and Captain Hobson was to confer with the Governor
of that colony in all matters relating to appointment
of subordinate officers and finance, while the Governor and Legislative Assembly were empowered to
establish a separate judicial system for New Zealand
and to pass any laws that might be required for its
good government. It was also provided that no
convict settlements were to be established in New
Zealand, and no convict labour was to be used in the
colony's development. Captain Hobson arrived in
Sydney on the 24th December, 1839, and after con-
ferring with the Governor of New South Wales, and
receiving some final instructions from him, sailed for
the Bay of Islands on the 19th January, 1840, in
H.M.S. "Herald." He was accompanied by the subordinate officers appointed by the Governor of New

South Wales. H.M.S. "Herald" arrived at the Bay of Islands on the 29th January, 1840, and on the following day the Commission of Captain Hobson's appointment, and the Commission extending the limits of New South Wales were read at Kororareka. Immediately afterwards, Governor Hobson issued a proclamation which put an end to the acquiring of vast areas of land by private individuals or companies direct from the natives. The proclamation notified that in future the Crown would only recognise as valid titles to land derived from or confirmed by Her Majesty. This led later to a good deal of friction between the New Zealand Company and the officers of the Crown. Governor Hobson's chief duty was still to be performed, and that was to gain the acquiescence of the native chiefs to British Sovereignty. On the 5th February, 1840, he assembled a great number of chiefs and their peoples near Waitangi in the Bay of Islands. Through the mediumship of Mr H. Williams, of the Church Missionary Society, who acted as interpreter, he announced his mission to the assembled natives. A good deal of discussion followed, and Hobson adjourned the meeting to allow of the matter being further considered. On the following day, the 6th February, 1840, the memorable Treaty of Waitangi was signed by 46 head chiefs, in the presence of at least 500 of inferior degree. The Treaty was ultimately adopted and signed by 512 principal chiefs from all over the colony. The provisions of the treaty were embodied in three articles. Under the first the chiefs ceded the sovereignty of their dominions to Her Majesty. The second confirmed to the natives the full possession of their land, and gave Her Majesty the exclusive right of pre-emption over such lands as they might desire to alienate, and the third article extended to the natives the protection and privileges of British subjects. The Treaty has been well kept on both sides and has done much to foster the loyalty of the native race.

On the 21st May, 1840, the Queen's sovereignty was proclaimed over the North Island by virtue of the Treaty of Waitangi, and over the South and Stewart Islands by virtue of the right of discovery. A second proclamation, at Port Underwood, of 17th June, 1840, claimed the sovereignty of the South Island also by virtue of the Treaty. In August, 1840, it was thought advisable formally to hoist the British flag at Akaroa, in order to avoid complications with the French who had sent out the corvette "L'Aube" to establish a French colony at that place. The British ship sent post haste by the Governor on the arrival of the French at the Bay of Islands arrived at Akaroa some three days before the French vessel, whose captain on arrival recognised the validity of the British claims. Some French immigrants remained and their descendants are still to be found at Akaroa.

The Governor's next business was the choice of a site for the future capital of the colony. His first intention was to establish the capital at the Bay of Islands, and for this purpose he acquired land some four miles from Kororareka. The town was named Russell, but did not prosper. The name Russell was afterwards given to the old settlement of Kororareka, which it bears to this day. The locality was found to be ill-chosen, and in October, 1840, the Governor finally decided in favour of Waitemata, where the city of Auckland was laid out, and proclaimed the capital of New Zealand. This choice engendered a good deal of ill feeling between the New Zealand Company's settlers at Port Nicholson and the Governor, the former protesting strongly against the claim of their flourishing settlement being passed over in favour of uninhabited Auckland.

On the 3rd May, 1841, New Zealand was proclaimed an independent British Colony, and Hobson was appointed Governor and Commander-in-Chief. The dependency upon New South Wales was now at an end, and New Zealand was henceforth governed by her own Executive and Legislative Councils.

In dealing with a proud native race it is inevitable that disputes ending in bloodshed should occur, and the experience of the pioneer colonists in New Zealand was no exception to this general rule. The most potent causes which operated to bring the

British population into conflict with the natives were, firstly, the attempt to apply the principles of English Criminal Law to native conduct; and secondly, the wrangling over sales of land of disputed native ownership.

The first actual collision of note with the natives terminated in the Wairau massacre. The natives, under the chiefs Rauparaha and Rangihaeata, disputed the right of the New Zealand Company to certain lands at Wairau, and announced their intention of obstructing the survey. The Company persisted, and the natives pulled up the pegs, burnt the huts and drove the surveyors off the land. For this act an attempt was made to arrest the two chiefs on the 17th June, 1843. A confused skirmish (with loss of life), precipitated by the accidental discharge of a loaded weapon, took place, during which several whites escaped. The remaining whites laid down their arms and awaited the natives. Unfortunately for them one of Rangihaeata's wives had been accidentally killed in the *mêlée*, and this chief, enraged at her loss, put to death the whole of the prisoners. The natives dispersed, dreading vengeance, and commenced to collect on the other side of Cook Strait to resist punishment. The Government of the day wisely pardoned the natives on the alleged ground that although both parties were in the wrong, the whites were the aggressors.

The war in the north, known as Heke's war, which centred round the Bay of Islands came next. It was noted for the chivalrous conduct displayed by the natives in the campaign. Its origin was curious and its object even more so. In November, 1841, a revolting murder was committed by a young native chief named Maketu. The Government demanded his surrender from the natives, who at first refused but later, after much discussion, complied with the request. Heke had been one of the violent minority, and determined to pick a quarrel whenever occasion offered. Maketu was duly tried and executed at Auckland on the 7th March, 1842. This was contrary to native custom, under which compensation would have absolved the murderer. Heke waged war, not against the colonists, but against the British power typified in the flagstaff at Kororareka in the Bay of Islands. The pretext was a refusal by a colonist of compensation, due under Maori custom for an insult to himself. Heke was joined in the war by another chief, Kawiti, who sought vengeance against the whites for an accidental injury to a relative. The flagstaff was first cut down on 16th September, 1844, and subsequently on the 10th and 19th January, 1845, and finally at the sacking of Kororareka by Heke and Kawiti on the 11th March, 1845. It was not re-erected till 1858 when the descendants of the natives engaged in the war voluntarily set it up

again. After the taking of Kororareka the natives
retreated inland to their strongholds. Tamahi Waka
Nene, a loyal native, now took up arms on behalf of
the Government, and his action prevented the spreading of the rising and checked Heke's aggression.
Heke retired to his Pa (stronghold) at Mawke. Here
an engagement took place which ended in the repulse
of the British. Blood having been spilt, the Pa in
accordance with native custom was abandoned.
During the retreat Heke came into collision with
Waka Nene and suffered a defeat. The next engagement was the attack on the Pa at Ohaeawai. Here
the Government forces met with a decided reverse
and with serious loss. This Pa was also abandoned
by the natives who retired to Ruapekapeka Pa. This
Pa was captured while the natives were absent holding a service in the bush on Sunday, 11th January,
1846, and the war died out. On 26th January, 1846,
peace was made and a free pardon granted to the
natives.

While these many disturbances and minor squab-
bles were in progress, changes had been made in the
office of Governor. On the 10th September, 1842,
Governor Hobson had died, and from that date to
the arrival of his successor, Captain Fitzroy, on 20th
December, 1843, his colonial secretary, Lieutenant
Shortland, acted as administrator. Governor Fitzroy
was replaced on the 18th November, 1845, by Captain,

afterwards Sir George, Grey, who held office till 31st
December, 1853. During these periods colonisation
was going on apace. Wellington, on the shores of
Port Nicholson, the first settlement of the New
Zealand Company, had grown into a flourishing town
of many inhabitants. Wanganui had been founded
by the Company in 1840 and Nelson in 1841. The
New Plymouth Company had established a settlement
at Taranaki in 1841, and the white population was
rapidly increasing. In 1842 an association of lay members of the Church of Scotland opened negotiations
with the New Zealand Company for the purchase of
land in the South Island. The association later became
connected with the Free Church movement, with the
result that the settlement was founded by members
of that body. The Company's officers in 1844 selected
a site on what is known as Otago Harbour, where the
city of Dunedin now stands. Owing to the war in the
north, no active steps were taken until 1847, when
an expedition under Captain Cargill sailed for New
Zealand. The "John Wickliffe" from London, with
Captain Cargill on board, arrived at Otago on 22nd
March, 1848, and the "Philip Laing," which left about
the same time from Greenock, arrived on the 15th
April. These were the pioneer ships of the Otago
settlement.

The next settlement was also of a denominational
character. An association was formed in 1843 to

establish a Church of England settlement in New Zealand. Owing to the disturbances of 1845 the matter was dropped till 1847, when it was revived. In 1849, owing to the energy of Mr John Godley, the Canterbury association was incorporated. In April, 1850, Mr Godley's party arrived at Port Cooper, now known as Lyttelton, and in December of the same year the first immigrants arrived.

In the year 1852 a new era began in the history of the colony. On the 30th June of that year the New Zealand Constitution Act was passed by the British Parliament, granting representative government to the colony. The history of constitutional government is treated of in a later chapter, and it is not necessary to do more than make a passing reference to the Act at this juncture.

From 1852 to 1860 the young colony made rapid strides, and a long period of prosperity was optimistically predicted. But unforeseen troubles arose which were to arrest its progress, saddle it with a deadening weight of debt, and force it to the verge of bankruptcy. The trouble arose through the ignorance of the Governor and the Colonial Office of Maori custom regarding the ownership of land, and the disregard of such custom by those having the ear of the Governor. The war which blazed forth over the Waitara purchase was the beginning of bloody conflicts with the Maori, which lasted intermittently for over ten years, and cost the colony many valuable lives and some millions of money. The troubles would probably never have arisen had the Colonial Office had the good sense to decide that the Governor was to be bound in native affairs by the advice of the members of the New Zealand Cabinet, instead of stipulating that he could disregard their advice at his discretion. Discontent had been prevalent for some time, and the great tribes in the Waikato had banded together to resist the sale of further lands to the Government, and, in order to cement their union, had appointed a leading chief, Te Wherowhero, afterwards called Potatau, their king. This federation was known as the King movement, and the Waitara dispute gave the opportunity to the natives to assume the aggressive.

The ten years' war may conveniently be divided into three periods. The first, from 1860 to 1861, during which fighting took place in Taranaki, arising directly out of the Waitara dispute; the second, from 1863 to 1864, commencing in the Waikato and closing in Tauranga with the final crushing of the King movement; and the third, from the first rising in 1864 to the final defeat of the fanatical Hau-Haus in the latter part of 1869.

The dispute with the Ngatiawa tribe over lands at Waitara was of long standing. The New Zealand Company claimed to have bought the disputed land so far back as 1840. An award had been made in the Company's favour by Mr (Commissioner) Spain in 1844, but was not accepted by Governor Fitzroy. The Ngatiawa chief, Wiremu Kingi Te Rangitake, had then stated that the natives would never part with the land. Disputes continued up to 1860, when a lesser chief of the same tribe claiming, as it was proved afterwards, without foundation, to be entitled to sell a block of some 600 acres, arranged a sale with the then Governor, Colonel (afterwards Sir Thomas Gore) Brown. Te Rangitake reiterated his former statement, and warned the Governor that any attempt to take the land by force would lead to war. The Governor unwisely directed Colonel Gold to occupy the land, and it was surveyed under military protection. On 15th March, 1860, the natives pulled up the pegs and erected a Pa on the land. The British force on the 17th attacked this Pa, but were repulsed. The natives, however, retired to Omata Pa, which Colonel Gold attacked on the 20th of the month, but owing to being outmanoeuvred by the natives withdrew his troops at dusk. The Pa was surprised and captured just at nightfall by Captain Cracroft with a force of bluejackets and marines from H.M.S. "Niger." At a Maori meeting held at Ngaruawahia in April of the same year, the King Potatau defended the attitude taken up by Te Rangitake, and Rewi, the chief of the Ngatimaniapoto tribe, shortly afterwards joined the fighting. The natives, hopeless of obtaining justice, petitioned the Queen to recall the Governor. Colonel Gold meanwhile remained on the offensive, and carried out some abortive movements ending in his repulse at Puketakauere Pa, which the natives had erected near the British camp at Waitara.

Major-General Pratt now succeeded to the command of the reinforced troops, but made no impression on the Maoris, who abandoned their Pas and took to guerilla bush fighting. About this time great alarm was felt in ungarrisoned Auckland at a threatened attack by the Waikatos, but the King-maker, Wiremu Tamihana Te Waharoa (William Thomson) held the natives back. In October, General Pratt had some success, taking three Pas near the Kaihihi river, and in the following months of November and December defeated a reinforcement of Waikatos at Mahoetahi, and again at Matarikoriko, where he captured their Pa, while he also repulsed an attack on a British redoubt near Kairau. Following up these successes he advanced to Te Arai. Here Te Waharoa, to whom Te Rangitake had transferred his rights to the Waitara land, intervened, and a peace was made on terms particularly burdensome to the natives. They included a provision that the disputed land should be surveyed and its title investigated. In January of 1861 General Cameron succeeded General Pratt, who returned to Australia, and Governor Brown formed plans to crush the King movement in the Waikato. He was succeeded by Sir George Grey before his préparations were complete. The new Governor decided to consult his ministers on native affairs, and with their co-operation to endeavour to win back the regard of the natives and to establish a permanent peace. One of his first acts was to abandon the terms of peace imposed by his predecessor. He visited the discontented chiefs, and was well received. Upon investigation their right to the Waitara land was demonstrated, and it was decided to hand it back to the Maoris. At the same time the Governor decided to occupy the Tataraimaka block, and Colonel Warre took possession on the 4th April, 1863. Unfortunately this was done before the proclamation returning the Waitara land was promulgated. The natives ambushed some regulars at Oakura shortly afterwards, and war flared out once more. In 1863 the Governor decided to attack the Waikatos. Great excitement prevailed amongst the natives. All Europeans were expelled from the King country, and preparations made for an obstinate resistance. Luckily for the colonists the great tribes of the Ngapuhi and Arawa stood firm to their allegiance.

On the 4th June, 1863, Governor Grey left Taranaki in H.M.S. "Eclipse" for Auckland. General Cameron decided to go by land, and crossed the Karikaia river in face of desperate resistance, his advance being covered by H.M.S. "Eclipse." On arrival at Auckland, the Governor, by proclamation of 9th July, called on all Maoris between Manukau and Waikato to surrender their arms and take the oath of allegiance. Distrusting the whites, the majority of the natives under their chiefs, decided to migrate to the Waikato. A further Proclamation in similar strain, dated 11th July, was issued, and on 12th July General Cameron crossed the Mungatawhiri into what was known as the King country and encamped at Koheroa. These acts were accepted by the Maoris as a declaration of war. An advance was made on the 27th, and some desultory skirmishes took place. These aggressions drove many loyal Maoris to join the Kingites, and Te Waharoa, who until now had vainly striven for peace, determined on war. The Governor further incensed the natives by proclamations confiscating their lands. Over 9000 volunteers were raised in the South Island for the war. Skirmishing took place in both Waikato and Taranaki during the months of September and October. The Maoris entrenched themselves at Mere Mere, which General Cameron reconnoitred on 29th October, but considered too formidable to assault. He determined on a flanking movement, but the Maoris forestalled him, and retired to Rangiriri. This place was subjected to artillery fire and carried by assault on 20th November, severe loss being inflicted on the defenders. The majority of the survivors were taken prisoners, some escaping by swimming the Waikaiu lake. Ngaruawahia was occupied on 8th December. The Rangiriri prisoners were incarcerated in the hulk " Marion " in Auckland harbour, and their treatment served to increase the native distrust and to prolong the war. This overwhelming defeat practically put an end to the war in the Waikato, but trouble still smouldered in Taranaki.

In March, 1864, Colonel Warre, operating in Taranaki, captured Kaitake, and in April Ahu Ahu. It was in this year that the fanatical Hau-Haus were first encountered. Driven to desperation by the successes of the Government, the Taranaki natives, under a chief, Te Ua, who claimed to be inspired, promulgated a new creed which, under the name of Hau-Hauism, was to spread throughout the country, and to cause many years of strife and bloodshed. At first the members of this body considered themselves invulnerable, and displayed desperate courage in their military operations. A determined attack made by them on Sentry Hill, near New Plymouth, on the 30th April, was repulsed with heavy loss. Wanganui was threatened. The loyal natives at this juncture challenged the Hau-Haus to a fight on the island Moutoa, in the Wanganui river, and defeated them, thus saving the town.

In the Waikato, the British force passing by Paterangi destroyed Rangiaohia, which contained the Maori food supplies, and the natives were compelled to disperse to bush fastnesses. The Government were not content to make peace. More Maori land was confiscated, and this was resisted by the Maoris. They also complained of the treatment of the prisoners taken in war, though they were treated better than they would have been in an inter-tribal warfare. The natives, driven from the Waikato, gathered under Rewi, the chief of the Ngatimaniopoto, at Orakau, and determined there to make their last stand. They quickly threw up the usual Maori fortifications. The defending force was, including women and children, but 400 all told. The combined attacking forces amounted to over 1250. Brigadier Cary invested the place on 31st March. The Pa was subjected to a galling artillery fire, and saps were thrown forward. On the 1st April two assaults were valiantly repulsed. The Maoris, without water and with but a scanty supply of food, still resolutely defended their position. The following day hand-grenades decimated the besieged, and gun-fire silenced their fire and made a breach in their defences. To a demand to surrender they replied, " Ka whaiwhai tonu—ake—ake—ake " ("We will fight on, for ever, and ever, and ever"). A safe conduct for the women and children was offered, but the women decided to stand by their men. Two

more assaults on the 3rd were beaten back with loss.
While the British commanders took counsel, the
Maoris, recognising that they could not hope without
food and water, and with failing ammunition, to hold
their ground, suddenly, with their women and children
in the centre, boldly marched out through the breach,
but not to surrender. Two or three remained in
order to divert the besiegers, the rest, husbanding
their ammunition for the final encounter, pressed
forward and fought their way to freedom. The pursuit lasted six miles. Of the whole garrison but half
escaped. Peace could now have been made, but the
Government were determined to punish the Tauranga
natives who had fought with the Waikatos, and dis-
patched a punitive expedition to that district. The
natives determined to defend their country with the
same resolution displayed by the Ngatimaniopoto at
Orakau. They erected a Pa near the Tauranga Mission Station, known afterwards as the Gate Pa. On
the 28th April a skirmish took place at Matata, in
which the British and Maori allies were successful.
General Cameron invested Gate Pa on the 28th, and
opened fire on the next morning. By four o'clock in
the afternoon a breach had been made and an assault
was ordered. The Maoris, in earth-covered shelters,
poured a deadly fire upon the advancing force. Officer
after officer fell, and the troops broke in confusion
and were soon in headlong flight, followed by the

On the Manganui-o-te-Ao River—Wanganui River

victorious Maoris. The British loss was over 100
killed. The Maori loss was trifling. The General
decided to wait till the following morning to renew
the assault, but during the night the Maoris abandoned their stronghold. They retreated to Te Ranga,
where Colonel Greer attacked them on the 21st June,
1864. Their unfinished fortifications were carried at
the point of the bayonet. The defeat was crushing,
and shortly afterwards the miserable remnants of the
Waikato tribe submitted. This ended the struggle with
the Waikatos. The war might now have ended had
not the Government claimed certain lands at Waito-
tara on the west coast. This led to the Wanganui
campaign, commencing in January, 1865. The Maoris
were strongly ensconced in the Weraroa Pa, not far
from Wanganui, and General Cameron thought their
position too formidable to attack with the force at
his disposal. His outposts were driven in with loss
at Nukumaru, close to Weraroa. He avenged this
loss on 14th March at Patea, defeating the Maoris
with much slaughter.

Meanwhile the Hau-Hau fanaticism had been
spreading and its adherents stirring up the tribes.
The Rev. Mr Volkner had been murdered at Opotoki
on the 2nd March. The loyal Arawas, however,
attacked and defeated the Hau-Haus at Maketu
a week later, and there was peace on the east
coast.

Te Waharoa, "the King-maker," took the oath of allegiance on the 27th May of the same year. On the west coast the campaign had not been so successful. General Cameron and Governor Grey violently disagreed. The Governor determined to undertake the campaign with the aid of the volunteers and of loyal natives, and to attack Weraroa Pa. He successfully carried out operations which ended in the evacuation of the Pa on the 22nd July, and a week later relieved a force besieged at Pipiriki.

General Cameron left New Zealand for England, and was succeeded by General Chute. In September, 1865, further lands were confiscated in Wanganui and Taranaki. The Hau-Haus again became active on the east coast, and fresh murders were reported. The Government forces, aided by the Arawas, harassed them continually. Pua Pa, then Teho Pa were taken, and Pukemaire Pa was assaulted, but weather conditions prevented the accomplishment of its capture. The Government was ably seconded by Ropata Wahawaha of the Ngatipouri, Mohena Kohere and other chiefs. Pa after Pa fell into their hands, and finally the Hau-Hau stronghold at Onepoto. It was during these operations that Te Kooti was arrested on suspicion of intriguing with the Hau-Haus. He was deported to the Chathams, and with other prisoners remained there for some two years. It is said that nothing could be proved against him, and the mistake made then was the cause of his bloody vengeance in later years.

In January, 1866, the Government determined to stamp out all opposition to their land confiscation in Wanganui and Taranaki, and General Chute carried fire and sword through the country, capturing Pa after Pa and laying waste the natives' cultivated lands. On the 4th January he captured Okatuhu Pa, on the 7th took Putahi by assault, and stormed Otapawa some days later. He then marched to Taranaki across country behind Mt Egmont, turned south past Oakura, and on the 1st February destroyed Waikoko Pa. At Opunake he arrested Te Ua and some peaceful followers and destroyed Meri Meri, and on the 7th February arrived at Patea. His operations had made him cordially hated by the Maoris, and some of the settlers disapproved of his conduct during the victorious march.

The Maori war was now at an end, but for several years the restless Hau-Haus, under the leadership of Titokowaru on the east coast, and later under Te Kooti on the west coast, were to carry on an intermittent guerilla warfare against the whites. McDonell, operating on the west coast in the beginning of August, dispersed some peaceful Maoris who had collected at Pokaikai. In the following month he surprised Titokowaru and his hapu (sub-tribe) at Pungarehu. The Maoris escaped to Popoia, where they made a stand, repulsing McDonell's first attack, but ultimately, being driven out towards the end of October, retreated inland. About the same time Colonel Whitmore surrounded and defeated some Hau-Haus at Omaranui, near Napier, on the east coast. Things remained quiet during 1867. McDonell was stationed in the Tauranga district, where he met with some minor successes. In the middle of 1868 fresh trouble arose on the west coast at Patea, but an event of far more importance was the escape of Te Kooti and his fellow-prisoners from the Chatham Islands. Overpowering the guards, Te Kooti and his followers seized a schooner and by threats compelled the crew to carry them to New Zealand. They landed at Whareongaonga on the 18th July, and for the next three years were driven from pillar to post, retaliating by murderous raids when occasion offered. Chased by a superior force under Colonel Whitmore, Te Kooti was forced to give battle at Puketapu. The engagement was indecisive, and he made good his retreat to the interior. Meanwhile, on the west coast, McDonell was striving to crush Titokowaru. In August he surprised him at Ngutu-o-te-manu and destroyed his village. In the beginning of September he determined to attack the fortified position at Te Rua-arua. Disregarding the advice of his Maori ally, Kemp, he was ambushed while passing Ngutu-o-te-manu and defeated with loss. It was in this engagement that the gallant Von Tempsky, the leader of the Forest Rangers, fell. Colonel Whitmore, released from his chase after Te Kooti, now assumed the command against Titokowaru, but was repulsed at Moturoa. A few days afterwards, on the 10th November, Te Kooti descended upon Poverty Bay, massacring women and children, and then made good his retreat to his stronghold at Ngatapa. Ropata, with the loyal Maoris, now took up the chase of Te Kooti. On the 5th December he made a gallant attempt to storm Ngatapa, but owing to insufficient support had to withdraw. Not to be beaten, he again, in conjunction with Colonel Whitmore and Major Fraser, invested the place on 30th December, finally, on the 5th January, capturing the Pa. Te Kooti escaped. The scene again shifts to the west coast, where, in February, 1869, Whitmore and McDonell shelled Titokowaru from his position at Tauranga-ika, taking his camp on the Patea river, and drove him to Te Ngaire. Closely followed, he escaped to upper Waitara. The pursuit was finally abandoned, and the west coast trouble subsided. Te Kooti meanwhile had raided the Bay of Plenty, and made good his retreat to the Urewera country. In April he again appeared, capturing a Pa at Mohaka and murdering Europeans and loyal natives. Then, eluding his pursuers, he cut up some troops at Opepe and gained Lake Taupo. His overtures to the Maori king were coldly received, but he managed to enlist the sympathies of Te Heu Heu. Henare Tomoana now took the field against Te Kooti. They met at Turanga, near Taupo. The victory rested with neither side, but the loss of horses greatly hampered Te Kooti in his future operations. McDonell and Kemp now joined forces with Tomoana, and Te Kooti became little better than a fugitive. Defeated at Pourere, near Lake Rotorua, he took sanctuary in the territory of the Maori king, and was left unmolested for a time.

On the 9th November, 1869, Mr Donald McLean, the minister in charge of native affairs, met the Waikato and Ngatimaniopoto chiefs at Pahiko in the King country, and later in the same month another minister, Mr Fox, had audience with the Wanganui chiefs. The upshot was a settlement of differences, a better understanding for the future, and the making of a permanent peace. Another result was the disapprobation by the king and the leading chiefs of the violence of Te Kooti and his rabble, and the promise of assistance to bring them to justice. Turia Topia and Kemp now started from the west coast to seek Te Kooti, who vainly endeavoured to make his peace with the Government. They were joined by McDonell, and came into contact with the fugitive at Tapapa, but again his elusive cunning stood him in good stead. On the 29th January, 1870, he was heard of at Kurunui, from whence he moved to Paengaroa, then south to Rotorua and Ohau, and finally to the Urewera country. Ropata again became active. Meeting Kemp at Ohiwa, together they followed the trail. Te Kooti swooped down on Opape, but shortly afterwards Kemp captured his stronghold, Maraetahi Pa. Ropata, pursuing, fell in with the fleeing band at Waioeka river and took many prisoners. The Urewera allies of Te Kooti then made their submission. Te Kooti once more suddenly raided the coast in July at Tolago Bay. This was his last outbreak. For the next two years he hid in the mountains inland from Opotiki, and then quietly escaped to the King country, where he was left unmolested.

The history of the colony now becomes a record of its industrial and political progress. The old days of war scares and alarms have passed away, and the present generation live in peace and quiet, and find the strife of life not in the pioneer struggle for existence and liberty, but in the ever-increasing complexities of modern civilisation.

CHAPTER III

THE MAORI

WHEN Tasman touched at New Zealand in 1642 he found there a native race whose prowess he had good reason to remember. These natives, or Maoris as they are called, are a branch of the same Polynesian race which inhabits the islands of the Pacific Ocean from Hawaii in the north to New Zealand in the south, and from Samoa in the west to Easter Island in the east. It is a matter of speculation whether these Polynesians were the first actual inhabitants of the islands of New Zealand. In his interesting book, *Maori and Polynesian*, Dr J. Macmillan Brown advances a theory that the Polynesians, on their arrival, found the islands occupied by the descendants of a primitive fair race, and he adduces evidence to show that this race was a neolithic Caucasian people whose migration can be followed from the Atlantic to the Pacific—across Siberia to Japan—by means of the megalithic monuments erected to their dead. This megalithic track he follows from Japan through Micronesia and Polynesia to New Zealand. He also mentions a black race, but this latter will be accounted for later as the previous Polynesian adventurers with traces of Melanesian admixture who came direct from Fiji. His theory, though fascinating and bold, cannot yet be considered as more than an interesting speculation, but he has opened a new field for investigation which, if delved into, may yield abundant hidden testimony to solve the riddle of the birthland of the human race.

Much has been written and many diverse views have been held concerning the original home of the Polynesians. Mr Percy Smith, in his *Hawaiki, the original Home of the Maori*, places the homeland of the Polynesian race in India, and his view is the one accepted by most modern writers. It is still a moot point, however, whether the Polynesians are an Aryan race or whether they are the descendants of a race driven to seek new lands by the pressure of the Aryan advance into India. Whichever hypothesis is correct, there is no doubt that the race, if not Aryan, has been greatly influenced by contact with the Aryans, and its language, customs and beliefs all show strong traces of this influence. The cradle of the race seems to have been either the basin of the Indus or the valley of the Ganges. In his book Mr Percy Smith gives a table of approximate dates in Polynesian history calculated from Rarotongan genealogies, and there seems no reason to doubt that the table is as scientifically accurate as it can possibly be made.

The dates given in this chapter are taken from his table, and the writer acknowledges his indebtedness to Mr Smith's scholarly work.

The Polynesian religion shows no trace of Buddhist influence, and this is of importance in fixing the date of the great migration. It is an ascertained fact that the period from 500 to 400 B.C. was a time of great unrest in India, and the placing of the date of the Polynesian migration at about that time is probably accurate. The route followed by the people was round the coast of Burma to Java, thence through the Celebes by the north coast of New Guinea, the Solomon Islands, and the New Hebrides to Fiji. First Java and then Fiji seems to have been a resting place, but the continuing pressure from behind drove the race onward. Tradition states that the race was living in Fiji about 450 A.D., but it seems to have been there for a considerable period anterior to that date. It was about this time that colonies were first planted in Samoa and in the Tongan group. As there is not space in this chapter to follow the various branches of the race in their migrations, it will suffice to state that about 600 A.D. the wanderers spread east to Tahiti and thence north to Hawaii and further east to the Marquesas and Easter Island, and about 300 years later south-west to Rarotonga.

It is difficult to say when the first Polynesians settled in New Zealand. In the year 650 A.D.

Ui-te-rangiora, starting from Fiji, made many long adventurous voyages of discovery. This was a period of great activity in navigation, and it is probable that between 650 and 800 A.D. there was some colonisation direct from Fiji. This would account for the Melanesian strain amongst the Maoris, for there is no doubt that the naval activity was caused by Melanesian pressure, which finally drove the Polynesians out of Fiji. A further evidence supporting this supposition is that cannibalism, as practised by the Maoris, is of Melanesian origin, and did not come with the last migration from Tahiti. Tradition speaks of a visit to New Zealand by a certain Maku in 850 A.D. After this date navigation declined for a space, but a second period of activity radiating from Tahiti began about 950 A.D., and lasted for some hundreds of years. New Zealand was visited in 1150 A.D., and later by Kupe and other seafarers during a period from 1250 to 1325 A.D. In the year 1175 the Chathams were settled by the Moriori from New Zealand. This people are Polynesians, descendants of those left by the first voyagers.

In 1350 A.D., owing to inter-tribal disputes in Tahiti and the surrounding islands, a large number of Polynesians migrated in a fleet of canoes to New Zealand. The canoes of the fleet were Tainui, Tokomaru, Te Arawa, Kurahaupo, Matatua and Takitimu. They made land off the East Cape, and from there

dispersed along the coast. The Aotea arrived at
about the same time from Ra'iatea, and the Mamari
is stated to have arrived shortly before. It is from
the islanders who came with this latter migration
that most of the present Maori tribes claim descent,
but there is no doubt that they were not the first
colonisers of New Zealand.

The Maoris are a race of medium height, broad,
sturdy and well proportioned. Their skins are a light
brown, sometimes not much darker than the southern
Italian or Spaniard; their hair usually a dark brown,
though there are instances of families with red hair.
Unlike the natives of Fiji and New Guinea, their
hair is straight or wavy, not curly. In feature, except
for a slight fulness about the lips and the breadth
across the nostrils, they are strangely European. In
some instances a Semitic cast of countenance is
met with, and often a lofty, intellectual brow. In
disposition they resemble children, having their con-
servatism and respect for ancient law and custom,
and allowing themselves to be swayed by the passion
of the moment. Proud, vain and arrogant, they easily
take offence, and never rest satisfied until an insult is
avenged. They are affectionate to their children and
respect the aged. In warfare cruel and crafty, the
quarrel over they bear no ill-will to their quondam
enemies. Mentally they are alert and quick at
learning, but in the time of their first contact with

Europeans were a prey to superstition and believers in witchcraft (makutu). Instances are known and reported of healthy persons dying from no other apparent reason than because cursed by some wizard or tohunga.

The division of labour between the sexes was similar to that amongst other primitive peoples. The women were the household drudges, the cloth makers, and attended to the provisioning and the cooking. Their position was little better than that of slaves, but they were well treated, and in many cases women of high ability were looked up to and revered by the tribe. The men were the warriors, hunters and fishers, the canoe and house builders, and the makers of nets, from all of which occupations the women were excluded.

The morality of the race was high. There was no marriage ceremony, only a handing over of the bride, but in spite of this, misconduct after marriage was extremely rare and universally censured. Strange to say, before marriage a certain amount of freedom was allowed, and did not militate against a girl's chance of matrimony.

In religion they were polytheists, with a tendency towards mysticism. Their mythology shows a decided resemblance to that of the Greeks and the Scandinavians. They have an elaborate story of the creation and also an account of the flood. They

Maori Women

believed that the spirits of the departed ones winged their flight to their paradise and were there judged according as their owners had lived. The later accounts of their old religious beliefs have been highly coloured by the missionary biblical teaching, and it is difficult to sift the old from the new. Christianity, as the faith of a superior race, with its teaching of peace and goodwill to men and its doctrines of the resurrection and immortality, appealed to their love of chivalry and their belief in immortality, and has gradually driven out the old superstitions and beliefs.

The observance of religious ceremonies was in the hands of a priesthood, and the learning and practices were handed down from father or grandfather to son or grandson. Women took no part in religious services. Omens were taken before the performance of any event, great or small, and played an important part in everyday life. Incantations were the prelude to all important actions.

By far the most potent and important factor in their religious and tribal government, however, was their system of *Tapu*. It is difficult to define *Tapu*, but it may be stated to be the making sacred of any person or thing. The breaking of the Tapu rendered the culprit liable to be punished by sickness and death sent by the gods, and also to be deprived of his property, expelled from the tribe by the people,

Maori Whare (House), Rotorua

and probably done to death if the gods' vengeance should be too slow. The fear of punishment by the gods was more potent than the fear of human castigation. Men might be deceived, the gods never. The best example of Tapu was the sanctity which attached to the person and property of a chief. Everything a chief possessed, his clothes, ornaments and weapons, became endowed with this mysterious quality, and it meant death to whosoever should tamper with his belongings. It is related by the Rev. R. Taylor, a missionary who spent a lifetime amongst the Maoris, that a chief Taonui lost his tinder-box, which was found and used by several men. These poor creatures, so great was their superstition and belief in the Tapu, died of fright on finding out to whom it belonged. Such examples might be multiplied did space allow. The priests or chiefs might tapu anything, the kumara plantations, the hunting grounds, a tree to be used for canoe building; and the sacredness imparted was more protection than an army of warriors.

It is impossible here to do more than draw attention to their superstitions and beliefs. Much that is interesting has been written by abler pens, much that, to the student of religions, is well worth patient study.

Their houses, built of reeds or wood, were oblong in shape, of small area, with an inverted V-shaped

Maori woman weaving Flax Mat

roof of considerable pitch, with long overhanging
eaves. There was one small door and one window.
A hearth of stone was situated in the end near the
window, through which, in the absence of a chimney,
the smoke escaped. The people slept on straw, rushes
or scrub of some description. The cooking was done
out of doors, in some districts in the natural hot
springs, in others in ovens. The Maori oven was a
circular hole dug in the ground lined with stones. A
fire was built on the stones and removed when they
were hot. The food was then placed upon the heated
stones and covered up with earth until ready for use.
The food of the Maoris consisted mainly of fish and
vegetable products. The kumara or sweet potato, the
taro and the fern root were their vegetables, birds
and dogs their meats, and, after Captain Cook's visits,
in addition the pig. The kumara and taro were cultivated, and were brought with them from the South
Sea Islands. Berries of different kinds added variety
to their repasts.

Their clothes were manufactured from the New
Zealand flax, the fibres of which were woven with
some skill into various patterns. The work was done
by the women, entirely by hand, there being no loom
even of the most primitive description. Other mats
were made of feathers of birds, and many beautiful
specimens of their very fine work are still in existence. Dog skins were worn by chiefs, and utilised to

decorate other garments. The Maoris were fond of ornament, and especially prized those made of greenstone. Only one or two garments were worn. They

Maori woman at Hirangi

were oblong-shaped; one was wrapped or fastened round the waist, and the other fastened across the chest under the right arm and over the left shoulder. In war only a small loin-cloth was used.

In the men the hair was usually tied in a knot on the top of the head and ornamented with a comb and some feathers. The women left it flowing or gathered it at the nape of the neck similarly ornamented. Earrings of stone were common, and sometimes the nose was pierced and a feather or piece of stone penetrated it horizontally. The main decoration, however, was the tattooing or the working of patterns on different portions of the body, especially upon the face. There were two kinds of tattooing, the Moko-kuri or straight line variety which is found in other Polynesian islands, and the Mata-ora, called after the traditional originator, or spiral tattooing. The latter is peculiar to the Maoris and is not found elsewhere, and is highly artistic in design. The operation was performed by cutting the skin with sharp shells and rubbing in a preparation of soot and oil. The effect produced was rather terrifying to European notions, but was considered a mark of beauty among the Maoris. Women were tattooed on the lips and chin, black lips being thought an especial attraction. One reason given for the tattooing of the lips in women was that the process by stiffening the lips enabled them more easily to hide their emotions. The custom seems to have originated in the wish to make a warrior more terrifying and determined-looking to his enemies,

A Maori Chief showing tattoo

and, in a race of warriors, thus became in the man the mark of renown and in the woman the criterion of beauty.

It is only natural that the descendants of such intrepid navigators should retain something of the racial skill in nautical matters. The art of navigation itself became partially lost through disuse, but their naval architecture improved owing to the finer timber to be found in New Zealand. Their canoes were built of one log, sometimes eighty feet in length, the beam being about one-tenth of the length and the depth about half the beam. To give extra free-board a plank, usually in one piece, was fastened on each gunwale. No metal fastening was used, the ties being made of flax fibre plaited into ropes. The prow was ornamented with a grotesque figure-head, and the after-end by an elaborately carved stern piece standing perpendicularly several feet high. Sail was only used with a fair wind, and consisted of a flax mat hoisted on two pole masts. The usual mode of propulsion was by paddles some six to eight feet long, with a pointed spade-shaped blade, which were used with a dipping motion. As many as 150 men were often carried in a large war canoe. The steering was done by paddles wielded by two coxswains, one sitting on each after-quarter. The top streak was elaborately carved in the larger canoes, and the whole canoe painted black or red-ochre with pointings of white.

Maori carving, done with their primitive stone implements, was a combination of grotesque distorted figures and spiral curves. The figures usually had protruding tongues, crooked limbs and eyes of pawa

Carved end of a canoe

shell, a material like mother-of-pearl. This carving was used to ornament their houses as well as their canoes. The execution was often rough and faulty owing to the inferior tools, but the completed design was pleasing and symmetrical.

The dancing and music of the Maoris resemble those of other Polynesian peoples. To an European their music sounds rather weird and discordant. It is set in a minor key, and the range, though small, is divided into quarter tones, which to our ears give a sensation of flatness. Maori voices are often soft and musical, but their native use of quarter tones gives them a predisposition to flatness when singing European music.

The dance was used by warriors as a preliminary to combat in war. The war dance, often erroneously called the Haka, and intended to signify defiance to their enemies, consisted of making the most hideous grimaces to the accompaniment of the waving of the arms and weapons and the beating of the ground with the feet, the whole keeping time to an incantation and gradually working up to a pitch of frenzy. The Haka proper was originally danced by the women to encourage their warriors, and was symbolical of the rewards that awaited the victors. It was danced in the kaianga or village prior to the setting out of the war party. There were other dances, some performed by women, but in no instance do the feet play the principal part, the body and arms always being the main factors.

The Maoris were past masters in the art of oratory. Their use of metaphor was carried to an extreme, and the poetry of their diction approached the sublime.

It was part of the education of a chief that he should be able to rouse his countrymen by voice and gesture to deeds of courage and determination or to acts of mercy and compassion, and in a race whose passions swayed their every act no leader could disregard this

Maori Carver at work, Whakarewarewa

accomplishment. To the sacredness with which they were endowed by Tapu, to the fame they acquired by feats of arms and to their powers of oratory the chiefs owed their *Mana*. We have no English word which accurately expresses the meaning of this Maori term.

Mana can best be defined as "the divine right of kings." The chief, by exercise of his mana, vetoed or consented to the sale of tribal lands. This mystic influence gave him the power of life and death over his people, gave him supreme jurisdiction in criminal matters or civil disputes, and made his voice all-powerful in councils of war. The combination of Tapu and Mana contributed largely to the establishment and maintenance of the moral and civic welfare of the race.

In the foregoing pages the Maoris have always been spoken of not as a nation but as a race. National unity they had none. The race was divided into tribes, at whose heads were the chiefs and priests, these two offices often being held by the same individual or individuals. These petty divisions were their weakness, and led to bitter intestine wars, which often ended in the destruction of whole tribes. Their land-ownership was communistic. Only the chief could bargain and sell, but he did so on behalf of the tribe. The only title to land was occupation. A tribe that could not hold its own was forced to migrate to land less rich or to fight its way to ownership against some weaker brethren.

The tribes usually had strongholds or *Pas* adjacent to centres of population, to which the natives could retreat when raided by their enemies. These Pas were strongly palisaded and trenched, and many of them showed a high degree of engineering skill. On more than one occasion in their conflicts with the British troops the Maoris repulsed storming parties of soldiers with heavy loss. They chose their sites

Maori carving

judiciously, and seldom indeed could the Pas be commanded from surrounding elevations.

As one would expect in a race whose main business was war, they were skilled in military tactics.

Before the advent of Europeans and the introduction of guns their arms were spears, axes and clubs (meres), all adapted for fighting at close quarters. These weapons were manufactured out of wood, bone or stone, and were often worn as ornaments in times of peace. They had various modes of fighting. One was to utilise a wedge-shaped formation to break the enemies' lines in a similar manner to the Macedonian and Roman use of the phalanx. On other occasions they would form up in masses and discharge their weapons at short range, taking advantage of any disorder in the opposing ranks to charge and complete the rout. Against the British they used ambuscades. On some occasions these could be utilised without the Maoris showing themselves, but on others it was necessary to attack with part of their forces, and by retiring draw the opposing forces into a cleverly planned trap.

It was on the occasion of an inter-tribal victory that the Maoris indulged in cannibalism. It was a superstition among them that by this practice they gained the valour of the vanquished. Especially was it the custom for chiefs who slew opposing chiefs to pick out and eat the eyes of the victim, in order to gain additional prestige and add to their Tapu and Mana. Chivalrous as they were according to their lights, in warlike operations no quarter was as a rule given to the conquered, and death, or at least slavery, was certain.

Such was the Maori race at the coming of the white man. What is the condition to-day and what its hopes for the future? The old generation of fighting men has passed away, and the destructive influences of what is worst in our civilisation have

Maori carved house with grotesque figures

sadly depleted the remnants which survived the tribal and European wars. At the end of the eighteenth century the Maori population was estimated at about a quarter of a million. It is now but a little over forty-seven thousand. The change from the strenuous life of their ancestors has made the race indolent and degenerate, and content to subsist upon rentals from their lands instead of working the lands themselves, a course which would conduce to their material, moral and physical advantage. There are signs that the youth are awakening to the fact that in work, and in work alone, lies the salvation of their race. The young Maori party are persistently striving to keep before their countrymen this truth, that only by unflagging endeavour can they hope to turn the tide of decay which threatens to engulf their people. Under its guidance an attempt is being made to train the younger generation in agricultural and pastoral pursuits, and to induce the Government of the day to allow a certain number of their brightest youths to become cadets on the Government's experimental farms. Already there are in the neighbourhood of the East Cape several sheep runs managed and worked entirely by Maoris. At these stations the facilities for handling the sheep and the machines for shearing are equal to those used by the best and most scientific European pastoralists. In addition to this, some members of the race who have graduated from our medical school are doing their best to combat disease by improving the sanitation of the Maori villages, and by spreading a knowledge of the best means for its prevention and the most efficacious remedies for its cure.

Maori village, Ohinemutu

CHAPTER IV

SECTION I

GOVERNMENT

A. GENERAL GOVERNMENT

IN 1838 the Secretary of State for the Colonies wrote that it was not the intention of the British Government to annex New Zealand. The agitation in England for the settlement of her surplus population in a country where the English flag was flying, the arrival of settlers from Sydney, the visits of whalers, the coming of English missionaries, and the activity of the French forced the Government to alter its expressed determination. In 1839 Captain William Hobson was sent to New Zealand as Lieutenant-Governor. He arrived on the 29th day of January, 1840, and the next day proclaimed British sovereignty. New Zealand was nominally a part of New South Wales, and Captain Hobson was under the control of Sir George Gipps, the Governor of that colony. The Governor and Legislative Council of New South Wales passed certain statutes dealing with New Zealand affairs, such as an " Act to empower the Governor of New South Wales to appoint a Commission with certain powers to examine and report on claims to grants of land in New Zealand," and an act relating to customs duties. A nominated Legislative Council was appointed in May, 1841, and in the same month an executive of three members.

The first meeting of the Legislative Council was held some weeks later, and its first ordinance was an act to declare that the laws of New South Wales, so far as they could be made applicable, should extend to and be in force in New Zealand, and the second and third ordinances were to repeal the acts of New South Wales passed to deal with New Zealand affairs. The only other acts passed in the first session were to establish courts, both criminal and civil, and an act to prohibit the distillation of spirits in New Zealand.

In 1846 the Imperial Parliament passed an act to confer representative government on New Zealand. It authorised the issue of letters patent to establish municipal governments, to divide the colony into two or more separate provinces with separate lieutenant-governors, and assemblies consisting of a Legislative Council and a House of Representatives, and to create a general assembly for the colony consisting of a Governor, a Legislative Council and a House of Representatives. The act gave leave to delegate to the Governor powers to create these institutions. On the 3rd May, 1841, a proclamation had been issued stating that Her Majesty had been pleased to call the North Island New Ulster, the South Island New Munster, and Stewart Island New Leinster. Letters patent were issued and powers delegated to the Governor, then Captain George Grey. The Governor objected to bringing the Act fully into force, as he thought it would be calamitous to have representative government when the European population was so small, when the Maoris were disentitled to any share in the Government, and when so many land claims were outstanding. On receiving his representations the Home Government agreed with him, and an Act suspending for five years the constitution granted by the Act of 1846 was passed on the 7th March, 1848. This excited some bitter feeling among the settlers, but it is doubtful if any one would now say the Governor was wrong. Two provinces were afterwards proclaimed. From New Ulster the territory lying south of a line drawn from the mouth of the Patea river to the east coast was taken, and added to the province called New Munster, which included all the territory not in New Ulster. Two lieutenant-governors were appointed, one for each province, Major-General Pitt governing New Ulster, while R. J. Eyre, afterwards governor of Jamaica, held the lieutenant-governorship of New Munster.

In 1848 the Governor and the Legislative Council passed a provincial councils ordinance, which provided for the creation of provincial councils in the two provinces of New Ulster and New Munster. There was no Legislative Council for New Ulster, the Council for the Colony, which sat at Auckland, doing any legislative work that was required for the northern part of the country. The legislative output of New Munster was not large, eleven statutes only being passed. The nominated Legislative Council of the Colony continued to be the Parliament of New Zealand till 1852, when a new Constitution Act, granting representative government to New Zealand, became law, some sections of which still remain unrepealed. It was not obtained without great agitation in the Colony, and petitions to the House of Commons. Agents appointed by the colonists visited England to further their demands. These petitions, and the resolutions passed at the meetings of the settlers and the dispatches from the Governor (then Sir George Grey) show that there was considerable political feeling against the Governor, and urgent demand for representative government. It was not till 27th May, 1854, that the first Parliament met under the new Constitution. Provincial councils were, by the Constitution Act, established in the six provinces of Auckland, Wellington, Taranaki, Nelson, Canterbury and Otago. Superintendents (or provincial governors) had been elected and provincial councils chosen before the general Parliament met.

When the first Parliament assembled, members of the Executive Council, appointed by the Governor, were in office, and the House of Representatives made an immediate demand for responsible government. The Administrator of the Government, as he was called (Lieutenant-Colonel Wynyard), refused, and the House was prorogued without any agreement being come to between the House and the Administrator. The members of the first Executive Council were : Lieutenant Willoughby Shortland, Colonial Secretary ; Francis Fisher, Attorney-General ; and George Cooper, Colonial Treasurer. They were succeeded by Andrew Sinclair, William Swainson and Alexander Shepherd, who held office till 7th May, 1856, when, during the Governorship of Sir Thomas Gore Brown, responsible government was established.

No sooner had the Constitution Act been promulgated than there were found many strenuously opposed to provincial councils. These contended that there was no need for any provincial parliamentary councils, and that municipal local governing bodies were all that were requisite. Some of the centralists, as the opponents of the provincial system were called, predicted the weakening of the central government, and pointed to the principalities of Germany and to the small States of Italy (which they said had injured both Italy and Germany) as the patterns on which the provincial councils had been framed. There were others also—settlers in districts some distance from the capital of the province—who objected to be ruled from the provincial centres. In this manner originated two political parties, the centralists and the provincialists, which, down to 1876, were ever active in struggling for their ideals of government. In 1858 a new Provinces Act was passed. It permitted the formation of more provinces, and one leading centralist declared that this act would be the "sledge hammer" that would crush the provinces. It was not, however, the new Provinces Act that killed the provincial system. The centralist and provincialist struggle was often interrupted and temporary party alliances formed on the native question. The question of peace or war with the natives divided the provincialists and centralists, and local questions also broke up their alliances. Where was the seat of Government to be? Was it to continue in Auckland, or was it to be removed to a site on Cook's Straits?

The public works policy of 1870—a policy that made the general Government the maker of railways and roads and the promoter of immigration—was the real "sledge hammer" that crushed the provinces. The general Government absorbed the main revenue of the colony. It had control of the customs. In those days there was little direct taxation. In the North Island there was little land to rate, and therefore no land revenue to keep the provincial administration going. Little by little encroachments were made on the provincial functions, and finally, after a great struggle in 1875, an Abolition Act was passed. The provinces of Auckland and Otago remained loyally provincial, but in the smaller provinces the centralists carried the elections held at the end of 1875, and in the following year the provincial system came to an end. The fact was, and is, that the English people do not appreciate federal government. Unitary government is what they admire, but who knows but that in the immediate future England may see that a true federalism will be her salvation?

Many centralists who were most active in agitating for the abolition of the provinces admitted years afterwards that they had made a mistake. The provinces should have been kept and perfected, and not abolished. This every impartial historian must say, that but for the provinces there would not have been that simultaneous advancement at different centres which New Zealand alone among the colonies showed between the years 1848 and 1876. Even the province of New Munster was not without its uses, and those who had ever visited Otago, Canterbury, Auckland and Nelson and seen how in a few years the wildernesses were made habitable places, and all kind of

institutions established, will say that the provincial
administration was more successful than any administration the colony has ever had. When the progress
that the provinces of Canterbury and Otago, especially,
had made in the twenty-one years they had provincial
administration, is remembered, it is no wonder that the
provincialists even yet look back upon the destruction
of the provincial system as one of the greatest legislative blunders New Zealand has made. This may
without question be said, that the administration was
more effective and more economical than the system
that succeeded it, and the Parliaments that met in
New Zealand when the provincial system was in
existence have not been excelled, in the ability of
their members, by any that have followed them. The
provincial councils were training schools for politicians,
and as the Government was ever brought into close
touch with the people, the interest and intelligence
of the voters on all political questions were more
exercised than they have been since the abolition of
the local government system.

If the scheme of the constitution suggested by some
of those who advocated the provincial system had been
carried out, and the Legislative Council under the
constitution made an elective body, and especially if
its members had been elected by provincial councils,
there would have been no abolition. There seems in
all federations ever a contest between the central

Government and the States. The problem of how to maintain the present federal government of the Commonwealth of Australia may soon arise. In the States of Australia there are some constituencies even now clamouring for the abolition of the parliaments of the States. "Is not one parliament for five million people enough?" they exclaim.

The recognition of the benefits of federal government is still far from universal. It is not recognised in England, and South Africa has not a federal constitution. In New Zealand there are still many federalists. It is true New Zealand did not join the Commonwealth, but it was not distance that made the people of New Zealand refuse to enter into a Commonwealth with their Australian brethren. They dreaded the same agitation for centralism that they had experienced in their own country, and they were not impressed with the wisdom often displayed by a strong central government.

· The franchise qualification for the electors to the first parliament was as follows: Every man having a freehold estate in possession of the value of £50 above all encumbrances or charges, and of which he has been seised or entitled for six months before registration, or having a leasehold estate in possession of the clear annual value of £10 per year, held upon lease having at least three years to run, or who, having a leasehold of such value, has been three years in possession before the date of registration, or being a householder or a lessee of a tenement £10 in value or in the country of £5 in value.

After the influx of gold miners at the end of the fifties and the beginning of the sixties, miners were allowed to vote on production of their miners' rights or licenses to mine, which were issued on the annual fee of £1. The first Miners' Franchise Act was passed in 1860, and there were various amendments down to 1870. In 1875 a lodger was allowed to be registered as an elector if he had occupied in the same electoral district, separately and as a sole tenant for 12 months in any year preceding the last day of December, the same lodgings, being part of the same dwelling house, and of a clear value if let unfurnished of £10 or upwards, etc.

In 1879 the franchise was so extended that every male resident if he had attained his majority could vote. The freehold qualification was continued, the value of the freehold being reduced to £25 with or without encumbrances, and there was created the residential franchise, which declared that any man who had been one year in the colony and six months in the electoral district for which he desired to vote could be registered. Aliens were disqualified, but naturalisation has, however, always been easy of acquirement. The same year—1879—saw the term of Parliament shortened. From the commencement of

Parliament till 1879 the term of the House of Representatives had been five years. It was in that year made and has since continued to be three years.

A new Electoral Act was passed in 1893, and that Act was the first to create an equality of the sexes. Women had granted to them the same political rights as men, save that no woman could be elected as a member of Parliament. The freehold qualification was abolished, the residential qualification being the only one required. It was impossible thereafter to vote in more than one district, and all elections had to be held on one day. The ballot system was introduced in 1870. A ballot paper containing the names of the candidates is handed to the voter, who strikes out the names of the candidates he does not wish to vote for, leaving the name of the person of his choice. The electoral law was consolidated in 1908, but it remains as defined in 1893. In 1887 was passed an Act to provide for the division of the colony into electoral districts. The mode of providing for the redistribution of seats based on population was then carried, and with some modifications is still the law. Two commissions are appointed to consider the results of the quinquennial census, and how far the returns of the population affect the electoral districts. The two commissions meet and determine according to the population what number of districts should be allocated to the North, and what number to the South

Island. On the numbers being fixed, one commission sits and divides the North Island into the number of districts allocated, and the other commission does the same for the South Island. The basis is that of population other than Maori population. The Maoris have separate districts and members. Twenty-eight per cent. is added to the rural population, and on the basis of one member for a district, the respective islands are divided into electoral districts. The population of the districts, after adding the 28 per cent. for rural districts, must, as far as possible, be equal. Where it is not possible to get equality, an allowance by way of addition or deduction not exceeding 550 persons is made. The system has worked well, and all complaints about legislative gerrymandering have ceased.

The number of ministers must not exceed eight, but there may be in addition two paid members of the Executive Council, who must be Maoris or half-castes. The Governor is appointed by the Sovereign and usually holds office for six years, but there is no limit to the years he may serve. The Parliament at present consists (1) of a Legislative Council of 44 members, of whom two are Maoris. These members are appointed by the Governor on the advice of the ministers, and hold office for seven years. There is no limit to the number that may be appointed. (2) The House of Representatives consists at present of

80 members, four of whom are Maori members elected by four Maori electoral districts.   Every Maori of 21 years of age, male or female, can vote.   No one can be chosen as a Maori member unless he is a Maori or a half-caste.   At present a half-caste elected by a European constituency is a minister, and a Maori elected by a Maori constituency is a member of the Executive Council.

At the election of 1908 there were estimated to be in the various ordinary electoral districts 538,950 adult persons of both sexes.   Of these 537,003 were on the rolls, and 79·82 per cent. of these voted.   There were 81·11 per cent. of males on the rolls who voted, and 78·26 per cent. of the women.   In 1905, 82·23 per cent. of women on the rolls voted, but the vote was as low as 74·23 per cent. in 1902.   In some of the contests in 1908 the result was a foregone conclusion, and the political excitement was small.

B. LOCAL GOVERNMENT

An American writer has said that the "Town Meeting"—the smallest local government unit in the United States—has been more important in the States than even the President and Congress.   Even if this statement should sound extravagant, still much depends on local government.   The educating influence and the training to self-control, and to freedom, are of as much importance as the unifying of a race or people by a strong central government. It is the local government that makes for liberty and trains the people to govern. New Zealand, from its earliest times, has always had local government. If its political history be compared with the other Australian colonies, it will be found that its distinguishing feature has been the importance. of local control in many government matters. It has now two kinds of local government for country districts and two for centres of population. The former are called Road Boards and Counties, and the latter Town Boards and Boroughs. The larger boroughs are called cities, but the government of the cities does not differ from that of the boroughs. The name is the only distinction, and it is given not because a borough is the cathedral town of a diocese, but on account of its population. There are 111 counties, 199 road board districts, 109 boroughs, including five cities, and 48 town board districts. The ordinary revenue of all these local governing bodies from rates, licenses, and special taxes is about £1,300,000. There is further revenue derived from Government grants, goldfield duties, etc. If these extra revenues were added, the total revenues under the control of the local bodies would mount up to about three and a quarter million pounds. These local bodies have borrowed monies. The boroughs have been the main borrowers, the amount due by

the other local bodies being small. The total indebtedness of the boroughs is about six millions, and
that of the general local bodies and counties, road
boards and town boards, about £120,000. There are
also special local government boards, such as river
boards, drainage boards, harbour boards, water and
supply boards, rabbit boards, fire boards, etc. To
these it is not necessary to refer. The mode, however, in which hospital maintenance and charitable
aid are managed will be described later.

The Dominion is divided into counties, but five of
them are merely geographical divisions, without any
local government. Some of them are almost devoid
of a white population. The counties are divided into
ridings, and where there are road districts in a county
the ridings are so arranged as to include one or more
road districts. If a part of a county has no road
district, it is called an outlying district. The county
is incorporated and is controlled by a council, which
consists of not less than six nor more than twelve
councillors. A chairman is elected each year by the
council. The electors of councillors are all those
whose names appear on the valuation roll of any
district in the county in respect of rateable property,
or on the list of miners' rights, that is, those who pay
£1 a year for the right to mine for gold. There is
a plurality of votes according to the valuation of
property up to three votes. The elections are held

triennially. The functions of the County Council are to make and repair roads, bridges and ferries, to look after sanitation, drainage, licensing of vehicles, fire prevention, lighting, and harbour works where there is no harbour board; and the councils may also contribute out of their funds money for charitable institutions, local telegraphs and telephones, public libraries, mechanics' institutes, agricultural schools, rifle ranges, cemeteries, etc. Bye-laws may be passed by the councils concerning all those matters which County Councils control and aid.

Road board districts are really smaller counties, though some of these districts are larger than counties. Their existence is a relic of provincial administration. Some provinces had small road board districts, and did not desire to lose the small local government districts to which they had been accustomed, and hence the keeping of both these classes of local government bodies. The road board franchise is the same as that of the counties, and the functions of the boards are similar to those exercised by the counties. The members of a road board must be not less than four, nor more than nine, and the qualifications of electors are the same as those of counties.

In the boroughs there is a borough or city council, and a mayor. The mayor is elected by the electors, and not by the council. The council consists of not less than six councillors and the mayor, and not more than twenty-one councillors and the mayor. The electors are all persons, male and female, who own freehold land of not less value than £25, or who are rated for property, or who have been in occupation as tenants or sub-tenants for three months, if the rent is not less than ten pounds a year, or who have resided for one year in New Zealand and in the borough or a ward of the borough for three months last past before the 15th February in the year when application to be put on the roll is made and is a British subject by birth or by naturalisation in New Zealand. In the case of husband and wife, any qualification possessed by either of them is deemed to be possessed by each. The functions of the council are many and various. Councils have streets, drainage, lighting (gas and electric), trams, bridges, ferries, water-works, sanitation, water for motive power, fire prevention, workers' dwellings, markets, public libraries, museums, public gardens, etc., etc., under their control. And they may contribute funds for recreation, instruction, etc. More than one borough has a theatre. The power of legislation by bye-laws is extensive. The control of buildings is very large. One of the things that strikes a New Zealander on his visit to a European city is the absence of fire escapes. Every private house, as well as all public buildings, stores, shops, halls and theatres must have efficient means of fire escape. If a stranger walks down a New Zealand street he will see iron or wooden ladders placed on most houses as fire escapes.

Town boards are smaller municipal bodies suited to villages. If the village has not more than five hundred inhabitants it remains part of the county. A town board consists of not fewer than five and not more than seven members. The electors have the same franchise as county electors, and the organisation is similar to a county, with like functions and powers.

The rates that may be levied by all these local bodies may be on the capital value of the land, deducting all improvements, or on the capital value of the land and all improvements, or on the annual letting value of the land and buildings. In eighty-three local bodies the rating is on the capital value deducting improvements. In boroughs the maximum general rate that can be imposed is two shillings in the pound on the annual value, and $1\frac{1}{2}d.$ in the pound on capital value, or its equivalent on the unimproved value, that is, the amount that $1\frac{1}{2}d.$ in the pound would realise on capital value is the amount that can be levied on the unimproved value. In counties the rate is respectively one shilling in the pound and $\frac{3}{4}d.$ in the pound. Extra rates may be imposed for water supply, lighting streets, and public buildings, sanitation, libraries, drainage, hospitals and charitable aid. In road-board districts the rates are the same as in the boroughs, and the town boards have the same rates as the road boards.

Hospital and charitable institutions are managed by special local bodies. There are 36 hospital districts in the Dominion, and there are nine separate institutions that get special aid.

For every hospital district a hospital and charitable board is established and incorporated. In the hospital districts are several local government districts, such as counties, road districts, boroughs and town boards; and each of these local governing districts is called a contributory district. The hospital and charitable aid board consists of one or more representatives for each of these contributory districts. The Governor in Council determines the number of representatives from the contributory districts. The Governor may combine districts to elect representatives. The board consists of not less than eight nor more than twenty members.

The electors have only one vote, and are those who are electors of the members of the local bodies. The hospital and charitable aid board has the management of all hospitals and separate institutions, that is, institutions for orphans, aged poor or poor, in its district. A board may establish institutions such as hospitals, maternity homes, convalescent homes, sanatoria, inebriate homes, reformatory homes for women and girls, and charitable homes. There is power to establish separate institutions, that is, institutions of the class mentioned, managed and maintained by voluntary efforts, and by subsidies from the board. The board may also appoint local committees of persons not members of the Board to manage institutions.

The local bodies in the district contribute in accordance with the capital value of the rateable property in their districts. The Government gives the following aids: (1) Ten shillings in the pound on all devises or bequests. (2) Twenty-four shillings in the pound on all voluntary contributions of money, land, or other property, not being devises or bequests. (3) For every pound levied in the contributory local bodies, (a) one pound in respect of capital expenditure, that is, for erection of buildings, or for purchase of farms, or furniture, etc., but not for maintenance: and for maintenance (b) an amount based on two calculations, first on the wealth of the district, and second on the amount levied on the contributory districts. This is thus ascertained. The total property of land and buildings in a district is fixed by the valuation roll, and the census gives the population of the district. Dividing the total valuation by the number of people, the wealth per head is arrived at. The other consideration is the levy made by the board on the contributory districts. Suppose the wealth of the district was £190 per head of the population, and the levy amounted to two shillings per head, the amount of contribution of the Government would be twenty-two shillings and threepence in the pound on the levy. Again, suppose the wealth of the district was £449, with the same levy of two shillings per head the contribution would be seventeen shillings and threepence. Again, suppose the levy was four shillings, then the Government contribution in the two cases given would be 18s. 3d. and 13s. 3d. respectively. The system, therefore, gives proportionally less to wealthy districts than to poor districts, and it gives more to economical districts than to those which are less careful in their expenditure.

The board may give outdoor relief to the necessitous, but the board is not compelled in law to give any relief. No board can be sued for not giving relief of any kind.

This system, which, with some modification, has been in existence since 1865, gets rid of small poor law districts, and the resulting troubles of "settlements." The areas of hospital districts are large, and as a large share of the funds is contributed by the general Government, the burden does not fall on local rates alone. Further, as administered in the past, the boards continually force the able-bodied to shift for themselves, and with the aid of the Government labour bureaux work is found for them. There is one important provision in the statute, namely, that the cost of relief granted to any person is a debt due by that person to the Board, and may be recovered by action against the person so relieved. If the relief is granted to a minor, or married woman, the cost of such relief is a debt due by the husband of the married woman or father of the minor, as well as a debt due by the person relieved. The Destitute Persons Act makes the following persons liable to maintain a destitute person, namely, the father, step-father, grandfather, mother, stepmother, grandmother, children, grandchildren, and brothers, including their executors or administrators. The only provision as to "settlements" is that where a person receives relief from a board before he has resided in the district of the board twelve months, the board may recover the cost of such relief from the board in the district in which he last resided for a period of two years at any time prior to the granting of that relief, but if he has left the district for five years there is no claim. It will be seen from this short summary that in some respects the recommendations in both reports of the Royal Commission on the Poor Laws and Relief of Distress in the United Kingdom (Parliamentary Paper 4499, Session 1909) have been given effect to. Lunacy is dealt with by the general Government. All public lunatic asylums, called "Mental Hospitals," are under the control and are managed by, and at the cost of, the general Government. There is only one private asylum in the colony, and it is inspected regularly by Government officers.

No doubt mistakes may have been innocently made, but up to the present time not a single charge of corruption or fraud has ever been made against any of our municipal bodies or any of their members.

Several municipalities have in the centres amalgamated, so that we have a larger Dunedin, a larger Christchurch, a larger Wellington, and a larger Auckland than existed some years ago. There is, however, a tendency in outlying districts to subdivide these. Counties have increased by the number of 48 since 1876, and the system of fission has gone on in other local bodies. When the large number of local bodies is considered, it will be seen that some thousands of our people are engaged, without fee or reward, in managing our local concerns, and who can estimate the educative effect of such public service on the race?

Section II

THE JUDICIARY

Besides the Arbitration Court which is described subsequently in the chapter on Labour Legislation, and the Native Land Courts which are tribunals to determine the rightful owners of native lands, to grant probate to native wills and to deal with the succession to and partition of native lands, there are four classes of courts :

(1) Justices' of the Peace Courts.
(2) Magistrates' Courts.
(3) The Supreme Court.
(4) The Court of Appeal.

(1) The Justices' Courts deal with minor offences and with the investigation of serious offences, sending persons charged with such offences to the Supreme Court, if the evidence produced warrants such a procedure. Stipendiary magistrates generally preside in the Justices' Courts, and some cases can only be heard by such magistrates. There are 32 stipendiary magistrates in the Dominion.

(2) In addition to the criminal jurisdiction, the magistrates have civil jurisdiction. This is divided into three kinds, "ordinary," "extended," and "special." "Ordinary" includes actions involving breach of

contract or tort where the amount does not exceed
£100, but not cases of false imprisonment, illegal
arrest, malicious prosecution, libel, slander, seduction
or breach of promise of marriage; also actions for debt,
balance of partnership account up to £200, attach-
ment of debts up to the same amount and recovery
of specific moveable property, recovery of tenements
(if the rental does not amount to £105 a year), or
other cases where the value is not in excess of £100
a year; also interpleaded cases where the amount
involved does not exceed £100, and all cases where
parties agree in writing to leave the matter to the
jurisdiction of a magistrate where the case can be
tried by a magistrate, but not exceeding £200, and
the granting of a writ of arrest in holding to bail any
one about to quit New Zealand leaving one unsettled
claim in the ordinary jurisdiction.

The "extended" gives jurisdiction up to £200 for
the same classes of action, and in addition the settlement of disputes under the Building Societies Act.
Under the head of "special" is given jurisdiction up
to £200 in cases of false imprisonment, illegal arrest,
libel, slander or breach of promise, recovery of specific
legacy where the validity of the will is not in issue,
grants of injunctions, and for arrests of persons about
to leave New Zealand. The special jurisdiction has
not been granted to any magistrates. Magistrates'
courts in the chief centres are held every week and

frequently in other places. The procedure is simple, a plaint note and a bill of particulars being filed. If a defendant wishes to defend he must file a notice of his intention to do so, and in certain exceptional cases where special defences are raised must give the ground of defence relied on. There are about 35,000 criminal and quasi-criminal cases investigated every year by magistrates, including a few by justices of the peace, and about 25,000 civil cases heard. Appeals lie to the Supreme Court.

(3) The Supreme Court has all the jurisdiction the High Court of Judicature in England possesses. It deals also with divorce and bankruptcy and has an admiralty jurisdiction.

(4) The Court of Appeal hears appeals from decisions of the Supreme Court. There are six Supreme Court judges, and these judges form and constitute the Court of Appeal. One supreme court judge sits in Auckland, one in Dunedin, one in Christchurch and three in Wellington. They visit other smaller towns on circuit several times a year.

The Supreme Court procedure is much simpler than in similar courts of other countries. The plaintiff proceeds by writ of summons to which is attached a statement of claim, and the defendant files in reply a statement of defence. The cause is entered in the list of actions by means of praecipe and is then ripe for trial, there being no other pleadings. Points of law that may arise in these statements may be argued on special case before the trial of the action. Claims for prohibition, certiorari, mandamus, injunction, etc. are all by statement of claim without writ for the relief sought, and an injunction can also be applied for as part of the relief in an ordinary action. The costs are all according to fixed scale and are settled by the judge when judgment is pronounced.

The Court of Appeal sits thrice a year and generally for fourteen weeks in a year, and all cases are disposed of before the court rises. Criminal trials are held four times a year in the chief towns and three or four times a year in the smaller towns.

Trials by jury are as in England. In civil cases a verdict of three-fourths may be taken after three hours' consultation. In criminal cases the accused can peremptorily challenge only six jurors. Any further challenge must be for cause. A challenge for cause is almost unknown.

Section III

EDUCATION

That it is the function of the state to educate its children was recognised in the earliest days of the settlement. In those days, however, it was also recognised that the state had to concern itself with the religion of the people. In the second session of

the Nominated Legislative Council—New Zealand's
first parliament—there was passed an ordinance to
aid in the building of churches and chapels, and to
endow ministers of religion.   All religions were to be
endowed.   Happily this ordinance was disallowed.
The Home Government advised Her Majesty to veto
the bill.   That this veto was in accordance with the
views of the people may be proved by the subsequent
history of legislation in New Zealand, and by an
incident in the first meeting of the first House of
Representatives.   The first proposal made in the
House was, that according to the time-honoured
custom of the House of Commons, the House should
be opened with prayer.   This proposal was opposed
by some of the leading men in the House, because
they feared that such a practice might lead to the
Government having to grant some privilege to a
particular church.   In 1847 an Education Ordinance
was passed, and it was assented to by Her Majesty.
Its preamble proclaimed its object.   The preamble
reads : "Whereas it is fitting that provision be made
for promoting the education of youth in the colony
of New Zealand."   Powers were given to the Government to establish and maintain schools, and to inspect
schools, and to contribute towards the support of
schools otherwise established.   In the school cur-
riculum, "religious education," "industrial training"
and "instruction in the English language" were

compulsory. The schools that could be aided were
to be under the control of the Anglican bishop of New
Zealand, the Roman Catholic bishop, or other head
of the Roman Catholic Church, the superintendent
of the Wesleyan Mission, or the head minister of any
other religious body. The Government had not much
means in those days, and little was done for education, and no Education Office was started. Land
endowments were given to various churches, and
some secondary schools in connection with churches
still exist that are indebted to such endowments for
their main support. In 1854 the new constitution
came into force, and education became one of the
duties of the new Provincial Councils. Not till 1867
was the 1847 Ordinance repealed, and then by a
Native Schools Act which was passed to regulate
and provide subsidies for schools for Maori and half-
caste children, and had nothing to do with general
education.

The Provincial Councils undertook this task imposed upon them, and at once set about providing
for education. The systems adopted by the provinces
were not uniform. In a few of them aid was given
to church schools, but in the larger provinces the
schools aided were either undenominational, or secular. The provincial systems continued till 1877 when,
the provinces having been abolished in 1876, a
general system was established. The control and

management were vested in large boards. There were altogether twelve boards (now increased to thirteen) provided for, and under these boards were committees for educational districts, which means practically a committee for each school. The board had the general management, and the committees the local management of the schools. The education must be secular, no religious teaching being allowed in school hours, and the education is free and compulsory. This system with slight alterations exists now. There are two classes of schools, the primary or common schools, and the district high schools. The salaries of the teachers, and money for the administration of the schools, come from the Government. There are neither school rates nor school fees; and the school books are also free. The district high schools are primary schools with a secondary department or additional secondary classes. At the end of 1909 there were 152,416 pupils attending the primary schools and 4121 pupils attending native schools. There are 64 district high schools. The number of public secondary schools is 29. All of these are endowed by grants of land or aided by monetary contributions from the Government. Some of the schools take boarders, but the majority of their pupils are day pupils. In 1909 4856 pupils, namely 2911 boys and 1945 girls attended secondary schools. In addition 2207 secondary pupils attended technical day schools.

In some of these schools the boys and girls are taught together, but there are some wholly boys' schools and some wholly girls' schools.

The expenditure on secondary schools was £140,648 in 1909. Of this sum the Government contributed directly £46,428. There are secondary school scholarships given by the Government to primary pupils in the primary schools. These scholarships are gained by competition. In addition to these scholarships the Government provides free places for all boys and girls that attain a given standard by a certain age.

Technical colleges and schools to the number of 45 have been established. There are also 122 places at which recognised technical classes were held in 1908, and there are 150 technical classes in connection with these centres, and at these 122 centres 21,518 residents attend. The subjects include drawing, design, ornament, modelling, painting, architecture, domestic science, and various trades, etc., commercial subjects, also music and singing.

Examinations in connection with these technical classes have been held, conducted by the Board of Education, South Kensington, London, and the City of London Guilds Institute. In 1907 there were 582 candidates in the art and science examinations and 263 in the technicological examinations held by the London Institutions. The Government annual expenditure on technical schools and classes is about £78,000.

There are several mining schools, and elementary agriculture is taught in 471 primary schools.

There are many private and church schools not receiving any Government aid. In 1909 these had 17,930 pupils. One feature of the state system is that military training is encouraged. There were 14,686 cadets in 1909, there being 185 cadet companies, 111 detachments and 14 sections. The total number of children drilled is 143,580, but that includes physical exercises.

In 1867 a Native School Act was passed, and in later years the native schools system has been much improved and extended. In the native schools English is taught, and some industrial training is given. There were, in 1909, 4121 Maoris and half-castes attending these schools. There are also 4429 Maori children attending public schools and 215 attending mission schools. There are 303 at secondary schools, so that there are altogether 9068 Maori children under European instruction.

There is another class of school that has been of much service in New Zealand, and that is the Industrial School, as it is termed. It is a school for neglected children and for children who may have committed offences. There are seven state institutions of this class, and four Roman Catholic

institutions which receiye a Government subsidy at a
rate per pupil. There are altogether 2151 pupils at
these establishments or boarded out, and still under
control of the authorities.

The effect of education on the youth of the
Dominion may be gauged by the fact that all the
population of age, save a few that were not reared
in the colony, can read. The latest statistics are
that 83·5 of every 100 persons—men, women and
children—in the colony could read. Between the
ages of 10 and 40 only 2·55 per cent. could not read.
As the Dominion is yearly obtaining some immigrants
it may be said that all the native-born can read, and
though the system is secular, the number of prisoners
in proportion to the population has decreased since
1877, and, relatively to those born elsewhere, the New
Zealand-born is less criminal than those claiming
other countries as their birth-places.

In 1868 there began in Otago a discussion as to
the need of giving the young New Zealanders the
opportunity of university education. One proposal
was to endow scholarships and send the most brilliant
of secondary school pupils to the universities of the
United Kingdom. This proposal did not meet with
much sympathy. It was felt that the influence of a
university, if such an institution were established in
the colony, would extend beyond the students that
were taught within its walls. The Parliament of the

colony passed a University Endowment Act in 1868. It dealt with small reserves already made in the county of Westland for university purposes, and set apart 10,000 acres of confiscated lands in Taranaki and 10,000 acres of the same class of land in Auckland for university purposes, and made provision for the superintendents and Provincial Councils to set apart reserves for university purposes. In 1869 the Superintendent and Provincial Council of Otago passed an ordinance founding a University for Otago, and endowing it with pastoral lands. When the General Parliament met in 1870 a Colonial University Act was passed. The Act contained two clauses of importance dealing with the Otago University. It provided that if the Council of the Otago University agreed with the Council of the New Zealand University to dissolve the Otago University, then the New Zealand University should be established in Dunedin. The agreement had to be made within six months from the passing of the Act, the 12th September, 1870. The Council of the New Zealand University was not appointed till the 3rd February, 1871, and the appointments were not gazetted till the 18th February. The council was not called together till the 31st May, when the time for agreement with the Otago University had lapsed. The fact is that more than one minister did not desire any such agreement. Nothing could therefore be done under the statute regarding an amalgamation of the two universities. The Otago University, meantime, chose professors, and obtained for university purposes a fine building in Dunedin that had been erected for a post office. Its doors were opened to students early in July, 1871, and large numbers of students entered. It was fortunate in having secured the services of three able professors, and since its starting its career has been very successful. The New Zealand University had no colleges to affiliate to it, and began its career by treating secondary schools as university colleges.

In 1873 the Superintendent and Provincial Council of Canterbury founded the Canterbury University College, and the council of the college took steps to begin teaching, the college being opened in 1875. In 1874, before its teaching began, a new University Act was passed by the general legislature. It recognized that the University established under the Act of 1870 had not been satisfactory. It provided that out of the permanent annual grant of £3000, part was to be spent in the expenses of the University, and part to be used for scholarships. Since the passing of this Act half the grant has always been set aside for scholarships. The University of Otago agreed to affiliate with the new University and to forego its power to grant degrees, and the Canterbury College also affiliated, and soon afterwards the secondary schools that had been looked upon as teaching institutions for the University ceased to be so regarded. In 1879 a University Commission was appointed, and it recommended two more university colleges, one at Auckland and one at Wellington. It was not, however, till 1882 that legislative provision was made for the Auckland University College, and not till 1898 that a university college was endowed and founded for Wellington. These four teaching university colleges are all well equipped. There are in the Otago institution now 32 professors and lecturers. It has a Mining School, a Medical School, and a Dentist School. There are 15 professors and lecturers in Canterbury College which has an Engineering School; affiliated to it there is an Agricultural College with its separate staff of teachers. Auckland College has 14 professors and lecturers. It has a School of Mining and Music. Victoria College in Wellington has 19 professors, assistants and lecturers. One feature of Victoria College is its Law School.

The University's sole function is to frame programmes of studies, hold examinations, grant degrees and certificates, and award scholarships.

In the University and in all the colleges there can be no religious test, and men and women are on an equality. They attend the same classes in the colleges, and compete for the same scholarships. A large number of women have obtained degrees, and some of the university instructors are women.

In 1877 a Royal Charter was issued to the University, and a supplementary charter was issued seven years later. Degrees granted by the University were declared by the charters to be recognized as academic distinctions and rewards of merit, and to be entitled to rank, precedence and consideration in the United Kingdom and in the Colonies and possessions of the Crown as if the said degrees had been granted by any University in the United Kingdom.

Already 1493 degrees in arts, science, medicine, law and music have been granted, distributed among 1338 graduates. There are yearly 36 junior scholarships granted (10 junior University scholarships, 25 senior National scholarships, and 1 Taranaki scholarship) besides special scholarships awarded by the affiliated colleges. The holders of these scholarships must pursue their studies at one of the affiliated institutions. The number of senior University scholarships is 17, but sometimes not all of these are awarded. There is also an annual travelling medical scholarship, and there are also two University prizes. The University has an accumulated scholarship fund of about £35,000.

Considering the population, about a million, the number who enjoy university teaching is large. In 1909 there were 438 students in Auckland College,

559 in Victoria College (Wellington), 408 in Canterbury and 441 in Otago. There were at least 200 New Zealanders abroad obtaining university education, mainly in the United Kingdom. There are also students exempt from attendance at classes. This would make at least 2046 New Zealanders obtaining university education. This is a greater number according to its population than those engaged in university studies in the United Kingdom. Assuming the population of Great Britain and Ireland to be forty-four times as large as that of New Zealand there should have been 90,024 undergraduates in the home universities. According to the published statistics for 1909 there were, including evening students, not 50,000. France had in 1906–7, 38,197 university students in a population of about 39,000,000.

The total expenditure in education by the Government in 1909–10 was £1,166,000. This includes the expenditure of the central office on primary, secondary, technical and industrial schools, also schools for the deaf and dumb, the blind, the mentally defective and on university education. It does not, however, include expenditure from special endowments or private benefactions.

There are many educative agents at work besides the schools and colleges. The Dominion has 236 newspapers. Of these 66 are daily, 35 are tri-weekly, 25 bi-weekly, 68 weekly, three fortnightly, 37 monthly and two others at periods of less than a month. In all the chief towns there is always more than one daily paper, and if the papers are examined it will be seen that they compare very favourably with the papers published in Great Britain. Every large town has at least one free public library. There are also other public libraries, and no village of any size is without some reading-room or library. There are also many literary, debating and scientific societies. The New Zealand Institute, an important scientific society, is in Wellington, and there are allied with it seven scientific societies in other parts of New Zealand. Its volume of yearly transactions gives much scientific information. Books and pamphlets are continually being published in the chief towns, and there is an intellectual alertness that is highly creditable for so sparse a population. The sale of books and magazines, both English and American, is large.

CHAPTER V

SECTION I

SOCIAL LEGISLATION

NEW ZEALAND has gained some prominence by enacting certain measures in the nature of social experiments. It would be a mistake to suppose that these social improvements have all been made in recent years. They began early in her legislative history and have not yet ceased. Before responsible or representative government was granted, some experiments were tried. In the judicial system law and equity were fused. There was one procedure in her Supreme Court for all kinds of actions or suits, and the mode of invoking the aid of her highest judicial tribunal was simple and expeditious. In dealing with real estate her Conveyancing Ordinance, 1842, simplified the law and introduced several new rules in Real Property law. A mode of registering deeds was enacted in 1841, and in 1860 a Land Registry system was enacted that was the forerunner of the Torrens system now found in all the Australian Colonies. Many of her early legislators were men who hoped to see enacted the last suggestion of the group of politicians known as philosophical radicals. Reform however came slowly. The widening of the franchise and the basing of representation on population hastened no doubt the number of social improvements. But there were many anterior to electoral reform.

In 1872 a Public Trust Office was established which still exists. This office undertakes the duties of executor or administrator, or trustee of estates, and the business for the year 1908–9 showed that the office supervised the administration of 5019 estates of the value of £6,399,567. In 1869 a Government Annuities and Life Insurance office was established. The office has been exceedingly prosperous. Its accumulated funds are over four millions, and the number of policies extant in 1909 were 48,016 ensuring £11,151,094. State enterprise in Insurance was extended by the establishment of a fire department. The Post Office Savings Bank was established in 1867, and at the end of 1909 the funds to the credit of 359,714 accounts were £12,666,897. There are besides the Government office, private savings banks with funds of £1,398,512 to the credit of the depositors. The telegraphs and telephones have always belonged to the Government, and perhaps in no other country in the world is the use of the telephone so universal for both private and business purposes.

A small private telephone service has been established by the Ngatipouri tribe of Maoris in the Waiapu county, and is used by that tribe for communication among their villages.

In 1869, when the war was still unfinished, though peace was at hand, a public works policy was inaugurated by the general Government. Hitherto the general Government had dealt almost entirely with the general affairs, leaving railways, roads, bridges and even public buildings to the provincial administrations. A new policy was in this year inaugurated, and strange to say supported by many who were provincialists and were desirous of maintaining the federal system of Government that had done so much for New Zealand between 1854 and 1869. These people did not see that the increase of the powers and the functions of the general Government would ultimately lead to the abolition of the federal system and the absorption of the provincial revenues, and of the provincial powers and duties. All railways belong to the Government and are managed by the Government. The mileage opened for traffic is 2717.

Railways which had hitherto been started and previously controlled in several provinces became Government property.

In Europe and America the feeling that the State should loom larger in the life of the |people has been growing. The time was when there was left to

individual enterprise the construction of almost all
public works save the formation of streets and
bridges. Waterworks, gasworks, railways, insurance
companies, banks, etc., were all owned and controlled
by individuals or private corporations. Slowly but
surely the conviction has grown that those enter-
prises to be successful must become monopolies, and
as such should be owned and controlled by the State.
This view has had its development in New Zealand.
Not only are railways owned and managed by the
State, but the supply of water rests with municipal
corporations, and lighting has become almost entirely
the business of the local authorities. The extension
of the functions of the State in New Zealand has
perhaps gone further than in any other British
territory. Depots have been established in some of
the chief cities for the sale of coal from the State
mines, and all the necessary appliances have been
provided to make such sales effectual and profitable.
There are Government experimental farms and a
Government vineyard. The main thermal springs
are owned and controlled by the Government, and in
the main thermal district practically all the springs
are owned by the Government. The Government has
bathing establishments at Rotorua, Te Aroha, Whakarewarewa, Hanmer, etc., with medical officers in
charge who may be consulted at fixed fees by all
desiring their advice. The township of Rotorua is

managed not by ratepayers, but by Government officers, and the Government has provided electric lighting and sewerage for its inhabitants.

The water power of our rivers and streams is owned by the Government. In no country of its size is the water power so extensive and so little used. It is sufficient, even if we had no coal, to provide energy, firing and lighting for a people more than twenty times our present population. How it is to be utilised is still a problem, but it is not likely to be left to private speculators or syndicates.

Four maternity hospitals have been established— one in each of the large centres. There are various institutions that are used for such purposes where the mothers are unmarried. The ordinary hospitals number 64 and are all under local government control. There are no hospitals in New Zealand like the large private hospitals of the home land. All are Government institutions managed by councils elected by the citizens, partially maintained by rates, and supervised by Government inspectors. Charitable aid is also directed by local elected bodies, and there are various "homes" for the housing of the old and the poor. There are 13 charity homes receiving some aid from the State and there are also some other private institutions that open the door to the needy.

The total receipts for the year ending 31st March, 1909, of all hospitals, including the four maternity hospitals, was £277,266, of which the Government contributed £104,656, local bodies £76,359, subscriptions, donations, etc. £17,340, rents of endowments £6,482, fees of patients £31,724, from old age pensions £2,690, payments made by local bodies for patients £1,294 and other receipts £18,567. The total expenditure was £247,122. The expenditure of the public on the State charitable aid boards and benevolent institutions was £112,818. Of this sum the Government directly contributed £49,413, local authorities £40,774. The balance was contributed by voluntary subscriptions, rents from endowments, from old age pensions, etc. A scheme of old age pensions was established in 1898. The original Act has received several amendments necessary for the smooth working of the system. The persons entitled to pensions are those who are 65 years of age, who have resided in New Zealand continuously, with certain exceptions, for 25 years, who have not been during the past 12 years in prison for 12 months, or on four occasions for any offence punishable by 12 months or over, or been imprisoned for five years for any offence, or have been guilty of desertion of wife and children. They must have lived a sober and respectable life. In the year preceding an application the claimants' income must not reach £60, nor must he have deprived himself of his property to obtain the pension. The highest pension payable is £26 per annum.

The amounts paid have been during the past six years:

	Pensioners.	Amount.
1905	11,770	£195,475.
1906	12,582	£254,367.
1907	13,257	£314,184.
1908	13,569	£325,199.
1909	14,396	£336,760.
1910	15,320	£362,496.

The Government of New Zealand is a money-lender. It grants loans to local bodies, that is to counties, municipal corporations, road boards, etc. for the construction of roads and other public works. These loans have to be secured by a special rate and the amount that may be granted is limited. The rate of interest is $4\frac{1}{2}$°/$_o$ for 26 years, 4°/$_o$ for 32 years, $3\frac{1}{2}$°/$_o$ for 41 years. At the end of these terms if the interest has been paid regularly the loan is discharged. The Government also makes advances to private individuals on first mortgages of land under freehold or leasehold titles. The advance must not exceed three-fifths of the value of the borrower's interest in the land. On first class agricultural freeholds advances up to two-thirds of the value may however be made. No loan can be less than £25 nor more than £3,000. The interest is 5°/$_o$ and the sinking fund 1°/$_o$ for 36 years till the amount is paid off. Two examples from the loan table will show how the interest and refund is paid.

1st half year for £100—£3, that is £2. 10s. 0d. for interest and 10s. for refund ; Balance owing £99. 10s. 0d.

24th half year—£3, £2. 10s. 0d. for interest, 17s. 8d. for principal : amount owing £83. 16s. 5d.

The amount advanced up to the 31st March, 1910, under this system was £9,025,275 to 25,722 persons. Loans not exceeding £350 are also granted to workers, but no worker having a salary of more than £200 a year can borrow. The advance is on the land for the express purpose of building a house. The land on which the house is built must be given in security for the loan. A system of discharge by yearly payments in the nature of rents has been elaborated. The amount advanced to workers has up to the 31st March, 1910, been £1,032,325 to 4105 workers.

The "long hand" of the Government has been stretched to preserve the monetary credit of the Dominion in another direction. In 1894 it guaranteed the deposits of the Bank of New Zealand, and since then this bank has been a quasi-government institution. It has six directors, four of whom are appointed by the Government, and the Government holds £500,000 of its stock. The bank in 1894 was in a perilous position, but now its shares are at a high premium, and its career has been very successful since the protecting aegis of the Government over-shadowed it.

Legislation having for its object the reformation of offenders against criminal law is in force and is still being introduced. In 1886 a First Offenders' Probation Act was passed. It allows a judge or magistrate to grant "probation," that is, not to punish by fine or imprisonment, any person found guilty or who has pleaded guilty of any crime save the following : "murder, attempted murder, burglary, coining, corrosive fluid throwing, demanding money with menaces, extortion of money by threats of accusation of crime, placing an explosive substance to endanger life or property, rape, robbery with violence, any offence attended with irreparable or serious consequences, or endangering life or indicating in the opinion of the Court an established criminal intention on the part of the accused." The criminal must be a first offender, previous to his crime of good character. Of the 2113 persons dealt with under the Act since October, 1886, no less than 1770 had at the end of 1908 satisfactorily fulfilled the conditions of their probation. 116 were re-arrested for other offences. 46 have left New Zealand. The percentage of those who may be said to have reformed is 83·81 per cent., and 2·17 per cent. have left New Zealand.

The Inspector of Prisons in his latest published report says : "The primary objects of the Act were to place first offenders under surveillance and to give them an incentive to good behaviour, and thereby to check what might be the beginning of a criminal career without sending them to prison, and to save them from the contamination which is almost inseparable from prison life, and in this the Act is certainly effecting these objects."

The criminal is placed on probation, that is, he is set free : sometimes he has to pay the cost of his prosecution. He may be ordered to report himself to the probation officer at stated periods for a definite time, one, two, three or more years. He may also be prohibited from visiting any place where intoxicating liquor is sold, and he may even be restricted in his place of residence. Sometimes youths are prevented from visiting any town. During the time he is under these restrictions he is said to be on "probation," and a violation of any of the conditions will lead to his re-arrest and imprisonment.

Another mode of dealing with criminals is what is termed the "indeterminate sentence." This system was introduced in 1906. An habitual criminal is defined as one who has been twice convicted of a serious sexual offence, or four times of serious offences against the person or property, or six times as an idle or disorderly person or an incorrigible rogue. These persons on conviction may be declared habitual criminals, and on such declaration there is no release from prison unless upon a recommendation of a board the chairman of which is a judge. Last year a further provision was made for dealing with prisoners. In addition to or in lieu of a sentence of imprisonment a convicted person may by a Judge of the Supreme Court be directed to be detained in prison for reformative purposes for any period not exceeding ten years, and by a Magistrate if convicted before him for any period not exceeding three years. A large farm has been secured to try reformative treatment. If the number of prisoners in prison is examined and a comparison made with previous years, it will be seen that crime is not increasing. The rate of distinct convictions was 38·61 per 10,000 of the population in prisons in 1890 and only 33·63 per 10,000 in 1907. Attempts are being made to provide for the reformation as distinct from the punishment of criminals. There are camps of criminals sent out to afforest some of the waste places of the island, and for some years back a considerable amount of tree planting has been done, an average of more than 4,000,000 trees a year having been planted by prisoners. They live in these camps a freer life than if cooped up in gaols, and the effect of this mode of treatment has been beneficial to most of them. A better classification is also being attempted and special efforts are being made to train the younger prisoners at a separate gaol in habits of industry, self-respect and honesty.

In 1874 an Act to change the mode of descent of
real estate was passed which came into force on the
1st October, 1875. The act applied only to a male
person dying and leaving surviving a wife or child or
children. All the land of which such person should
die seised or possessed without devising the same,
went to his administrator as if it was personal estate.
This provision was extended by the Administration
Act, 1879. There is now no distinction between the
descent or distribution of real and personal estate.
In the 1879 Act there was a provision as to illegiti-
mates dying intestate leaving property. If a male
illegitimate dies intestate without issue, his property
goes to his widow and mother in equal shares. If
the mother is dead, it all goes to the widow, and if
there is no widow it goes to his mother or her next
of kin, excluding the father and all persons claiming
through him. In the case of a female illegitimate
dying intestate leaving no husband or legitimate
children or their issue, but leaving illegitimate
children, the illegitimate children or their issue
succeed as if legitimate. If she leaves no legitimate or illegitimate children or their issue and no
husband then it goes to the mother or the mother's
next of kin. Again, where a woman dies leaving no
husband or legitimate children or their issue, but
leaving illegitimate children, her estate goes to her
illegitimate children or their issue. The English

Statute of Distributions is also otherwise modified. Take, for example, the provision whereby if a man dies intestate leaving a widow and no children, and the net value of his estate does not exceed £500 it all goes to his widow.   If the property exceeds £500, she gets £500 absolutely and a share in the balance.

A Testator's Family Maintenance Act was passed in 1900, and two slight amendments were made in it before it was consolidated in 1908 with the Family Homes Protection Act under the title of the Family Protection Act.   Its provisions are : If any person dies leaving a will without making adequate provision for the proper maintenance and support of a wife, husband or children, the Supreme Court may in its discretion, on application by or on behalf of the wife, husband, or children, order that such provision as the Court thinks fit shall be made out of the estate for the wife, husband or children.   The sum may be a lump sum or a periodical payment.   Various powers are given to the Court to carry out this principle.

New Zealand has passed a law somewhat similar to that in force in Scotland for the legitimation of illegitimate children.   The first Act was passed in 1894 and with a slight modification is still the law.   It provides that any child born before the marriage of his or her parents (whether before the coming into operation of the Act or not), whose parents have intermarried or shall hereafter marry, shall be deemed on registration of the child as provided in the Act, to have been legitimized by the marriage from birth, and shall be entitled to all the rights of a child born in wedlock. It also provides that the child of any such child who dies before the marriage of his or her parents shall take by operation of law the property which would have accrued to such child if such legitimized child had been born in wedlock. If there existed however at the time of the birth of the child a legal impediment to the marriage of his or her parents, then the provisions of the Act do not apply. There is also a limitation as to property that became vested before the passing of the first Act in 1894.

A further law has been passed to favour and help children. It is the Adoption of Children Act. The first adoption statute was passed in 1881 and several amendments have been made since then. The Consolidation Act of 1908 provides that a husband and wife jointly, or a married woman alone with the consent of her husband, or an unmarried woman alone who is at least 18 years older than the child to be adopted, or an unmarried man at least 40 years older than the child may apply to a magistrate for an order of adoption. The magistrate hears the case in camera, and after taking evidence may sanction the adoption. If the child is over 12, the child's consent is necessary, and the consent of the parents or of the guardian is requisite if the child is not a deserted child. No premium can be paid to the adopting parent, and on adoption the child for all purposes, civil and criminal and as regards all legal and equitable interests, liabilities, rights and benefits, privileges and consequences of the natural relation of parent and child, is deemed in law the child born in lawful wedlock of the adopting parent. There are several ancillary provisions. Guardianship of children is also dealt with by statute. On the death of the father the mother becomes the guardian, either alone or jointly with a guardian appointed by the father, and in all applications for the custody of children the Supreme Court makes the welfare of the child the first consideration.

The marriage ceremony has to be performed by a Registrar of marriages or by a minister of a church duly authorised. Births, deaths and marriages must all be registered. Marriage with a deceased wife's sister was first legalised in 1890, and with a deceased husband's brother in 1900.

Married women have a Protection Act, first enacted in 1860 and extended by subsequent legislation. At present a married woman may hold property as a *femme sole* and may dispose of it as if she were unmarried, without the consent or intervention of her husband or any trustee. She may enter into contracts and sue and defend actions as if unmarried, and any damages recovered by her are her separate property. Her contracts are deemed to bind only her separate property, possessed by her or which may hereafter be possessed. There are various other minor provisions dealing with the law laid down in the general terms stated.

Discussion about trusts or monopolies has been heard in this land. The legislature has endeavoured to deal with certain monopolies, and in three separate years, 1905, 1906 and 1907, has framed statutes to control what are termed "trusts" formed to control the production or sale of agricultural implements, flour and other products. These statutes, now consolidated by the Monopoly Prevention Act, 1908, provide, that if two or more manufacturers of agricultural implements complain to the Minister of Customs that the price of any agricultural implement on importation has been materially reduced, and that competition on unfair lines has been carried on by the importers of implements from foreign countries, the minister may summon the "Agricultural Implement Inquiry Board." This Board is a creation of this statute and consists of the president of the Arbitration Court, the president of the Farmers' Union, the president of the Industrial Association of Canterbury, some person appointed by the Governor on the recommendation of the Trades and Labour Councils and some person appointed by the Governor on the recommendation of the Agricultural and Pastoral Associations. The

Board is clothed with power of inquiry as extensive as the Court of Arbitration, and it reports whether the price of the implements has been reduced below the current price, and may recommend relief.   If the manufacturers of implements in New Zealand reduce the price materially below the current prices a Board may also be summoned.   The relief that may be granted is a bonus to the manufacturers not exceeding $33°/_{\circ}$ of value so as to enable manufacturers to compete with imported implements.   Implements manufactured in the United Kingdom are deemed to be manufactured in New Zealand, so that it will be seen that "foreign" does not in this connection include the United Kingdom.   Power is also given to refund customs duties on materials for implements.   This provision dealing with implements only continued in operation till the 31st December, 1910, but has now been extended to 31st December, 1912. Though the Act has been in existence for some years there has been only one case under it, and no relief was granted.

The second part of the Act dealt with the preventing of an increase in the price of flour through a union of the flour millers, and also of wheat, potatoes and fruit.   No relief had been granted under its provisions when this part of the Act was repealed in 1910.   It gave power to the Governor to order an inquiry by the Arbitration Court if the prices of these articles are unreasonably high. The relief granted was to admit wheat, flour and potatoes free of duty. The duties imposed are, on wheat 9d. per 100 pounds, on flour 1s. per 100 pounds, and on potatoes £1 per ton.

Amendments have been made in the Divorce Law. No distinction is made between husband and wife as far as relief is concerned. Either husband or wife may obtain a divorce (1) for adultery, or (2) for desertion for five years, or (3) for habitual drunkenness for four years, when a husband is respondent if he has in addition during that period habitually left his wife without means of support or habitually been cruel to her, or when a wife is the respondent, if she has in addition habitually neglected her domestic duties and rendered herself unfit to discharge them, or (4) on the ground that the respondent has been convicted and sentenced to a term of seven years' imprisonment or upwards for attempting to take the life of the petitioner, or of any child of the petitioner or respondent, or (5) on the ground that the respondent has been convicted of the murder of a child of the petitioner or respondent, or (6) that the respondent is a lunatic or person of unsound mind and has been confined in a mental hospital for ten years, in a period of twelve years prior to the filing of the petition, and is unlikely to recover.

If the petitioner's case is established, unless the petitioner's habits and conduct contributed to the wrong complained of, divorce must be granted. If, for example, a woman who has been guilty of adultery sues for a divorce from her husband on the ground of his adultery, she is entitled to succeed unless her adultery can be said to have contributed to his, and so in like case if the husband sues, he is in the same circumstances entitled to succeed.

The social evils that beset the older countries of Europe are not absent from the British possessions beyond the seas. There is crime, there is vice, there is drunkenness, and there is indulgence in harmful drugs, wherever there are human beings. Has organised society a duty to look after the physical and moral well-being of the members of society? The New Zealand people through their parliament give an emphatic affirmative reply to this question. As has been pointed out, they are dealing with crime and with criminals; they have provided a secular education system in which ethics are taught; and they have entered on a crusade against the use of harmful drugs. These drugs have been attacked—opium, alcohol and tobacco. So far as opium is concerned, it is unlawful to import opium in any form suitable for smoking, and if any one does so he may be fined £500 and sentenced in default of payment to 12 months' imprisonment. Nor may opium in a form that can be made suitable for smoking be imported, save with the permission of the Minister

of Customs.   Opium may not be manufactured for
smoking, and its smoking is unlawful, and any person
who aids or abets the smoking may be punished.

As to alcohol there is no distillation of spirits
allowed.   There is also what is called a local option
prohibition of the sale of alcohol.   Every electoral
district, save the city electorates that are for this
purpose amalgamated, is a licensing district, the
licensing authority being a stipendiary magistrate,
and a committee of five persons chosen every three
years.   At every triennial election of members of
Parliament a licensing poll is taken.   At this poll
there are three questions put to the electors :
(1) Whether the number of licenses is to continue ;
(2) whether no licenses are to be granted.   A majority
of votes for continuance means continuance, but if
three-fifths of the votes cast are for no license, no
licenses can be granted.   If neither vote is carried
licenses continue.   In a district where no license
prevails a vote for local restoration is taken, the
voting paper being (1) for local restoration or local
no-license.   Before local restoration can be carried
three-fifths of the voters must so vote.   If there are
not three-fifths for local restoration the determination
of no-license remains.   This has, with some modifications, been the law since 1893.   In 1910 an amending
Act repealed a provision for taking a vote on the
question of reducing licenses, and enacted that a poll

for National Prohibition was to be taken at the usual triennial election. This vote will be taken in 1911. If three-fifths of the entire voters of the colony vote for National Prohibition, then in four years from the vote all licenses of any description to sell intoxicating liquors shall cease at the end of the licensing year, and the importation, manufacture, sale or possession of intoxicating liquor of any description is unlawful save in accordance with regulations to be made by the Governor for medicinal, scientific, sacramental or industrial purposes. In 1893 only one electorate (Clutha), consisting mainly of Scotch settlers, carried no-license. There are now twelve electoral districts under no-license, and at the last election the total for the whole colony was 414,292 valid votes cast, consisting of 235,554 men and 186,399 women. For no-license the vote was 221,471, for continuance 188,140, and for reduction 162,562. A voter can vote for more questions than one. There were before the last vote was taken 1364 licensed hotels and accommodation houses, 154 wholesale licenses, 72 packet licenses and 30 bottle licenses. Since the last vote there has been considerable reduction. The no-license vote has risen at every election since 1893. In 1896 it was 98,312; in 1899, 118,575; in 1902, 151,524; in 1905, 198,768 and in 1908, 221,471.

The amount of alcohol consumed per head of the

people was in 1909, including Maoris, 9·256 gallons of beer, 0·705 gallons of spirits and 0·136 gallons of wine. The consumption of alcohol per head is therefore about one-third what it is in the United Kingdom.

The sale of tobacco is not controlled except to prohibit the sale to youths under 15 years of age. Every person is liable to be fined who sells, gives or supplies any cigarette, cigar or tobacco in any form to any youth under the age of 15 years, and such a youth who smokes tobacco in a public place is liable to be punished.

With so many functions assumed by the State in New Zealand considerable taxation is required to meet the necessary expenditure. There has been a progressive increase in the rate of taxation imposed, and new taxes have necessarily been adopted that were unknown in the earlier days of the settlement. The main sources of revenue are the Land Tax, Income Tax, Death, Customs and Excise Duties. For the financial year ending 31st March, 1910, the total Government income from taxation amounted to £4,245,858, produced as follows :

Custom and Excise Duties　　.. 　...	£2,786,490
Land Tax ...　　...　　...　　...　　...	£642,270
Income Tax　　...　　...　　...　　...	£316,835
Death Duties　　...　　...　　...　　...	£192,014
Miscellaneous Taxes　　...　　...　　...	£308,249

The customs duties in the early days were few
and simply imposed. They were levied on intoxicating liquors, on tobacco, on coffee, on tea, on iron,
on salt, on wood. There were only two other taxes:

Class 1 : boots, shoes, apparel, jewelry, cutlery,
watches, plated ware, silk, woollen and linen goods
(corn and gunny bags and wool sacks free), and
candles, all at 3s. per cubic foot of outside measurement of the packages in which these goods were carried.

Class 2 : All other goods save those exempted,
1s. per cubic foot of outside measurement as in first
class or two shillings per hundredweight. This
system continued with variations as to the amount of
duty till 1866, when more specific duties were imposed, though many goods were still charged at a
definite rate per cubic foot. It was not till 1873 that
ad valorem duties were generally adopted, and since
then the tendency has been to increase the customs
duties, especially on goods that can be produced, or
manufactured in New Zealand. At present there
are sixteen classes of goods that pay duty and sixteen classes that are exempt. There are also six
classes of goods that come under the preferential
tariff. Customs duties are mainly for revenue producing purposes, although some of the duties are
protective in character. Many manufactured articles
that can be manufactured in New Zealand are free,
such as agricultural machines, mining machinery, etc.

These and other exemptions have been granted to foster local, pastoral, agricultural and mining enterprise. Tea is free if the produce of British dominions, otherwise it is liable to 2d. per pound. Coffee and cocoa are also free. Sugar is free. The duty on beer is 2s. per gallon : on spirits, cordials, etc. 16s. per gallon : on wine 5s. to 9s. per gallon.

The excise duty in New Zealand is a beer duty of threepence per gallon.

The Customs Laws give a preference to goods manufactured in or the produce of the British Empire. Tea, as already mentioned, is dealt with under the preference tariff. The goods placed in the preferential tariff are of six classes : (1) cement, Portland and other structural and building cement if foreign—that is, come from countries outside the British dominions —pays double the duty which cement produced in the Empire pays. (2) Certain other goods such as boots, shoes, candles, firearms, drain pipes, lamps, etc. pay 50 per cent. more duty than what may be termed Imperial goods of these kinds. (3) Foreign goods in this class pay 20 per cent. of the ordinary customs duties in addition. Some of the goods are matches, leather goods, machinery, electric fittings, etc., fish, cars, waggons, brush ware, etc., stationery manufactured, etc., etc. (4) Goods paying twenty per cent. of the value for duty, as defined by the Customs Law Act, 1908. Some of these goods are in the free

list if from the British dominions.   (5) Goods paying
ten per cent. of value for duty as above.   (6) The
tea duty of 2*d*. per pound.   It will be seen that sub-
stantial preference is thus given to the goods from
the Empire.

In order to levy a Land Tax all land in New
Zealand is valued, there being a capital value assessed
of land without improvements, and a valuation of the
improvements.   The Land Tax levied for 1909 was
1*d*. in the pound on the unimproved value of land,
and ¾*d*. in the pound on the mortgagee's interest in
the land, assessed as capital value of the mortgage.
In addition there is a graduated super-tax assessed
according to the following table.

Where the total unimproved value of all the land
of any taxpayer

is not less than	and is less than	the Graduated Tax is
£5,000	£7,000	1/16*d*.
£7,000	£9,000	2/16*d*.
£9,000	£11,000	3/16*d*.
£11,000	£13,000	4/16*d*.
£13,000	£15,000	5/16*d*.
£15,000	£17,500	6/16*d*.
£17,500	£20,000	7/16*d*.
£20,000	£22,500	8/16*d*.
£22,500	£25,000	9/16*d*.
£25,000	£27,500	10/16*d*.
£27,500	£30,000	11/16*d*.
£30,000	£35,000	12/16*d*.
£35,000	£40,000	13/16*d*.

If the unimproved value is over £40,000 but under £41,000, the tax is 8s. for every hundred pounds of the land value : for every additional £1,000 over £41,000 the percentage is increased by one-fifth of a shilling up to £200,000. Over £200,000 the percentage is £2 for every £100,000, so that for £200,000 unimproved value of land the tax is £4,000.

All land, pastoral, agricultural and suburban, is taxed. There is an exemption of land up to £500 in value if the unimproved value is not over £1,500, and up to £2,500 there is an exemption of £1 for every £2 of such excess over £1,500.

The Income Tax is as follows : (1) On the income of all companies and of all non-residential taxpayers (*a*) where the income does not exceed £1,250, one shilling in the pound ; (*b*) where the income exceeds £1,250 but does not exceed £2,000, one shilling and one penny; (*c*) where the income exceeds £2,000, one shilling and twopence. (2) Other taxpayers having been allowed a deduction of £300 from their income and a further deduction not exceeding £50 for life insurance premiums, are charged as follows:

Where the income does not exceed £400, sixpence in the pound, where it exceeds £400 but not £600, sevenpence, and so on, rising one penny by gradation up to one shilling where the income exceeds £1,000 but does not exceed £1,250. Where it exceeds £1,250 but does not exceed £2,000 it is one shilling

and one penny, but where the income exceeds £2,000
it is one shilling and twopence.

The death duties are as follows : On all property
real and personal upon the final balance of the
estate,

Not exceeding £100	No Duty
Exceeding £100 but not £1,000, on first £100 ...	No Duty
on remainder ...	$2\frac{1}{2}$ °/₀
Exceeding £1,000 and not exceeding £5,000 ...	$3\frac{1}{2}$ °/₀
Exceeding £5,000 and up to £20,000	7 °/₀
After £20,000 and any amount over that sum ...	10 °/₀
In cases of bequests or legacies to stranger in blood	3 °/₀

Section II

LABOUR LEGISLATION

The Legislature of New Zealand has dealt seriously
with the labour problem.   It would be a mistake to
suppose that labour legislation is a recent product.
The interference with employment dates back to 1873,
when a statute was passed entitled the Employment
of Females Act, 1873.   Its provisions were few.   No
female might be employed in preparing, or manufacturing, articles for trade or sale, not being contract
or piece work, between six in the afternoon and nine

in the morning, or for more than eight hours a day. All females were to have the following holidays without loss of wages, viz. Saturday afternoon from two o'clock, Sunday, Christmas Day, New Year's Day, Good Friday, Easter Monday, and any other day set apart as a public holiday. Every workroom was to be properly ventilated. The Act, it will be seen, limited the hours and days of labour, and provided for workrooms having fresh air. Various amendments were made: children were brought in, and Acts enlarging the provisions of the statute were passed in 1874, 1875, 1881, 1884 and 1885. In 1891 a Factory Act was passed, and all labour in factories, that of men and boys, as well as girls and women, was controlled. Various amendments in law have been made since the passing of the 1891 Act. The present law appears in a consolidated statute passed in 1908, and its main features are shortly the following: "Factory" is defined as a building, office, or place in which two or more persons are employed in any handicraft, or in preparing, or manufacturing, goods for trade or for sale. Laundries, bakehouses and boiler-houses are all included. "A boy" is defined as any male under 18, and "woman" means any female irrespective of age. All factories must be registered, and no factory can be registered that is not, in the opinion of an inspector, a suitable building for the work required.

The working hours provisions are: (1) No male

worker may be employed for more than 48 hours, excluding meal times, in any one week, nor more than eight hours and three-quarters in any one day, nor for more than five hours continuously without a break of three-quarters of an hour for a meal. Certain establishments are exempted, such as freezing works, dairy factories, fish curing works, jam factories, bacon factories and sausage curing factories. It will be noticed that these factories are what may be termed factories dealing with primary products, and related to pastoral, or agricultural, or horticultural operations. The persons getting up steam in factories for machinery are also exempted.

(2) No woman or boy may be employed for more than 45 hours, excluding meal times, in any one week, nor for more than eight and a quarter hours in any one day, nor for more than four and a half hours without the intervention of three-quarters of an hour for meal time. Women may not be employed between the hours of six in the afternoon and eight in the morning, nor boys between six in the afternoon and a quarter to eight in the morning.

A slight modification in the case of women and boys employed in woollen mills has been made, but it is only an increase to 48 hours a week and eight and three-quarter hours in any one day.

Overtime is allowed, but this may not exceed, in the case of women and boys, more than three hours

in any one day, nor overtime for more than two consecutive days, nor more than thirty days in a year,
nor on any holiday or half-holiday, etc. The age of
employment is restricted. A boy or a girl under 14
years may not be employed without special authorisa-
tion, and not in any event if more than three persons
are employed in the factory, nor may a girl under 15
be employed as a typesetter, nor may any girl, or boy,
under 16 be employed in doing grinding in the metal
trade, or in dipping matches of any kind, nor may a
girl under 16 be employed in making or finishing
bricks or tiles or making or finishing salt, nor any
girl under 18 where the process of melting or anneal-
ing glass is carried on, nor may a boy, nor a woman,
be employed in any room where the silvering of
mirrors by the mercurial process or the making of
white lead is being carried on. There are other
limitations of boy, girl and woman labour.

"Sweating" has been dealt with. If the occupier
of a factory lets out work of any description, in connection with textile, or shoddy material, he must keep
a record of the full name and address of the person
so employed, the quantity and description of the
work done, and the nature and amount of the re-
muneration paid for such work, and to the work
done ; a label on a prescribed form must be annexed.
If such label is removed before sale a penalty is
inflicted, and if any person to whom the work is given

sublets it a penalty is imposed. If a person employed in a factory does any work of the factory out of the factory he is liable to be fined, and also his employer.

There is a control over the wages. No one may be employed at a less wage, whether for piece work or not, than 5s. per week for the first year in the factory, 8s. a week for the second year, 11s. per week for the third year, and so on by additions of three shillings per week until 25s. per week, and then never under 20s. per week. These provisions are irrespective of overtime, which must be separately paid for. The wages must be paid fortnightly.

The holidays for boys and women are Christmas Day, New Year's Day, Good Friday, Easter Monday, Labour Day, Sovereign's birthday, half-holiday every Saturday from one o'clock in the afternoon.

There is special provision as to the sanitation of factories, and to prevent unhealthy persons being employed in any factory concerned in the making or canning of food, etc.

The hours, however, under the Factories Act may be further limited, and the wage increased, under the Industrial Conciliation and Arbitration Act.

A special statute deals with shops and offices. "A shop" is defined as any building, or place, in which goods are kept, or exposed or offered for sale, or in which any part of the business of a shop is conducted, but does not include a warehouse doing exclusively a wholesale business. "Office" means any building in which any person is employed directly or indirectly to do any clerical work in connection with any mercantile or commercial business or dealing. The following offices are excepted : solicitors', mining companies', miners' unions', or any building, or room, in which the clerical work of a factory or shop is carried on, if situated in a factory or shop.

The hours of employment of shop assistants vary. The closing hours are from 6 p.m. in the case of butchers' shops to 11.45 p.m. in the case of refreshment rooms, but shops in the boroughs must close at 1 p.m. one day in the week, and not later than 9 o'clock on one evening and at 6 p.m. on all other evenings. All shops are closed on Sundays. No female assistant in any shop, wherever situated, can be employed later than 9 p.m., except on Christmas Eve and New Year's Eve. Even an occupier's family, if shop assistants, cannot work longer hours than other assistants. The number of hours a shop assistant may work is limited to not more than 52 hours, excluding meal times, in any one week, and to not more than nine hours, excluding meal times, in any one day, save on one day, when 11 hours, excluding meal times, may be worked. There are many ancillary provisions to carry out these limitations of hours. Shops must be closed on one working day in the week at 1 p.m., but the day chosen may differ in different districts.

Wages must be paid at intervals not longer than a fortnight, and wages must not be less than 5s. a week for the first year of work, mounting up by three shillings each week for each year of service till the age of 20 years is reached. No employee can pay a premium to be employed. Certain shops, fishmongers, fruiterers, confectioners, refreshment room keepers, bakers and chemists are exempted from some of the general restrictions as to hours that have been mentioned.

In 1894 an Industrial Conciliation and Arbitration Act was passed. There had been, in 1890, a disastrous maritime strike, and it was urged that some such provision as then existed in Massachusetts of having an officer, specially charged to bring about peace between employer and employees, might be tried. But what if the attempt at conciliation failed? A bill had indeed been drafted in South Australia in which there was to be recourse to conciliation or arbitration with a sanction. If the parties would not, or could not, agree, an agreement was to be made for them, and this agreement enforced. It was on these lines that the New Zealand Industrial Conciliation and Arbitration Act was drafted. Most of its leading features are still the law under the Acts of 1908. Under the 1894 Act and its amendments (and there were amendments in the following years: 1895, 1896, 1898, 1900, 1901, 1903, 1904, 1906 and 1908), the principle of invoking a Court, if conciliation fails, of compulsorily setting wages, hours of labour, and conditions of labour for employees, in various industries remains. At one time the conciliation principle was most in view, and at another time the Court of Arbitration settled all disputes. The Conciliation Boards were not very successful. The provisions of the existing Act, as amended by an Act passed in 1908, may be summarised as follows: The colony is divided into industrial districts, and there is a Council of Conciliation for each district. There are four Conciliation Commissioners. A Council of Conciliation consists of the Conciliation Commissioner for the district, and assessors, who may be one, two or three, appointed by those who apply to the Council to intervene in a dispute, and a like number appointed by those who are called the respondents, and who are engaged in the trade in the district where the dispute originates, and who are either employees if the employers appeal for the settlement of a dispute, or employers if employees are the complainants. There is provision for registering unions—that is, unions of employees in a certain trade, and associations of employers engaged in a trade. If any dispute arises between the employees of the trade and the employers, either party may apply to the Council, and the Council can then sit and hear the dispute. If the Council is unable to get the parties to agree, the Council tries to get a temporary agreement sanctioned till the Court of Arbitration can sit and hear the dispute, and the Arbitration Court deal subsequently with the dispute. The Court consists of a judge who is also a judge of the Supreme Court, appointed for life, and one assessor elected by all the trades unions of the Dominion, and one elected by all the employers' industrial associations in New Zealand. The Court has power to settle any dispute, and to determine the length of time an award may be binding, not exceeding three years. It has to decide according to equity and good conscience as it thinks fit, and from its award there is no appeal to any tribunal. Its function is more legislative than judicial, for it fixes wages, hours of employment, and the conditions under which an industry has to be carried on. An award cannot increase the statutory hours of labour, but it may limit them, and it may also increase the wages provided by statutes for employees.

In the year ending 31st March, 1909, there were twelve industrial agreements made (which, on being filed, had the force of awards), nine recommendations made by Conciliation Boards, which also had the effect of awards, and 88 awards made by the Arbitration Court and other Courts. So there are still labour disputes in New Zealand, but they are usually settled without strikes and lock-outs.

So far as strikes and lock-outs are concerned the present provisions were enacted in 1908. "A strike" was defined as the act of any number of workers, who are or have been in the employment, whether of the same employer or of different employers, in discontinuing that employment, whether wholly or partially, or in breaking their contracts of service, or in refusing, or failing after such discontinuance, to resume or return to their employment, the said discontinuance, etc., being due to any combination, agreement or common undertaking, whether express or implied, made with intent to compel employers to agree to the terms of employment asked by the employees, and to injure the employers or to procure another strike, or assist other workers in the employment of any other employers.

"Lock-out" means the act of an employer in closing his place of business, or suspending, or discontinuing his business or any branch thereof, with intent to compel or induce any workers to agree to terms of employment, or comply with any demand made upon them, by the said or any other employer, or to cause loss to his workers, or to procure another lock-out, or to assist any other employer, to compel or induce any workers to agree to terms of employment or comply with any demand made by him.

The penalty on a worker, if there is any award in his industry, is not exceeding £10, and on an employer a penalty not exceeding £500.   If a worker, not himself striking, instigates or aids or abets in a strike, he is liable to a £10 penalty, and an industrial union which aids, etc., is liable to a penalty not exceeding £200.   Any person who gives money to a party to strike or lock-out, or to a union of workers or of employers of which a striker or one who causes a lock-out is a member, is deemed to have aided and abetted a strike, or lock-out, and is liable to the penalties already mentioned.   If the majority of a union, employees' or employers', has engaged in a strike or lock-out, the union is held to have aided and abetted the strike or lock-out.   There are special and increased penalties for strikes and lock-outs in such special industries as gas, electricity for light and power, delivery of coal, water supply, slaughtering of meat, working of ferries and tramways, etc.   There are also many provisions for punishing breaches of awards or of industrial agreements.

There are special provisions for the hours of labour and wages of coal and gold miners.

There are also many stringent provisions as to the conduct of coal mining.   No female or boy, that is, a male under 13, can be employed in or about a coal mine, and the employment of youths between the ages of 13 and 18 is much restricted.   They cannot be employed as ladder or bracemen at a place set over a shaft, nor have charge of an engine, or windlass, or of any part of the machinery, ropes, chains, tackle, etc., by which persons are brought up or carried along in a mine, nor for more than 48 hours in a week, nor for more than eight hours in a day, except in cases of emergency. Persons in charge of steam machinery are limited to eight hours' consecutive work, and then a rest of four hours must intervene.

A miner is entitled to overtime when he is employed underground for more than eight hours a day, and under the award under which coal miners work this means wages at an increased rate. There is no Sunday labour save by permission of an inspector, and permission must only be given when the work cannot be suspended without risk to the mine. There are multitudinous regulations as to ventilation, ways, keeping of explosives, etc. There are also provisions for compensation to workers for accidents, and an accident is declared *prima facie* proof of negligence.

The Crown may resume all coal-bearing land which has been alienated by the Crown since 1891, but the owners have to be paid compensation for the land and improvements, but not for coal. In every mine there is a sick and accident fund for the relief of miners or their families, and the employer has to pay one halfpenny per ton on all coal except brown coal or lignite, and a farthing a ton on brown coal or lignite. The money is paid in to the Government savings banks, and the Minister of Mines and the Public Trustee are "trustees of the fund."

There are somewhat similar provisions enacted as to gold mining. No female and no male youth under 14 years of age can work in or about a gold mine, etc., and there are elaborate rules and regulations as to the conduct of gold mining, similar to those enacted by the Coal Mines Acts.

The care of the State is not, however, confined to miners. The employer has, under a penalty, to provide proper accommodation for agricultural labourers and sheep shearers. Seamen also have not been neglected. The Government sees that proper accommodation is provided, and the Arbitration Court fixes the rate of wages. In fact, over all labour there is the *aegis* of the Government. There is even a Scaffolding Act to guard the lives of builders. There are workers' dwellings erected by the State in many parts of the Dominion, and as has been pointed out, loans are granted by the State to workers who wish to erect their own houses.

In 1908–9 there were 12,040 factories registered, the hands employed in factories were 78,848, and the wages paid £5,710,226. There are 12,689 shops, and in these shops 34,119 persons are engaged. Of these,

11—2

20,701 are shop assistants and the remainder are employers. £1,792,199 were paid in wages to shop assistants in the year 1908–9.

There are 49,347 workmen belonging to 345 trade unions, and 3918 employers belonging to employers' unions.

The total number of industrial agreements and of awards in force is at present 354.

At the basis of the system of industrial conciliation and arbitration lies the recognition of trade unions and employers' unions, and the system could not perhaps be worked unless such a basis were recognised. It would be almost impossible to deal with individual complaints from either employers or employed. In those trades or occupations where unions are unknown, awards are unknown. There have been no awards in the case of domestic service, nor in the case of agricultural labourers, and the question has been debated whether domestic servants can be said to be workers in an industry in the meaning of the Act. In many industries a preference has been given to the employment of members of a trade union of the industry over those who are non-unionists. Where such a provision has, however, been inserted in an award, the award has almost always laid down the terms of admission to the union. All workers of the trade must be admitted on payment of a small annual fee.

It is continually asked what has been the effect of this interference with labour, this fixing of the wages, conditions, hours of labour, etc. Before an answer is given the particular and peculiar position of New Zealand must be recognised. It is a thinly populated country that exports but a small quantity of manufactured goods. Its main exports are the products of the pastoral and agricultural farms, and of the mine. Out of a total value of over 20 millions of exports, manufactured goods (if flax—*Phormium tenax*—be eliminated) show no sign of increase during the past ten years. In 1897 the value was £193,622, and in 1908 £176,039. The articles exported were ale, beer, apparel, leather, soap, woollens and miscellaneous. In most of the industries in which awards are made, the industries are not affected by outside competition. It does not matter what wages or conditions of labour prevail in the bakers' or butchers' trades, for example: fresh bread and fresh meat must be had by the inhabitants. A law that might be successful in New Zealand, which is not an exporter of manufactured goods, might wholly fail in a country that relied on its sale of manufactured goods to foreign peoples. This, at all events, can be said: strikes have been rare, and the Dominion is progressing. It is recognised that no industry is worth having if it cannot pay a living wage. The people in New Zealand believe that it is better to have no industries than to have a people steeped in

misery, with physical health shattered, and with no
hope of comfort or happiness.

There is one fact that may have some bearing on
the subject, and that is, that often wages exceed
those fixed by awards, and that when work is scarce
there are few applications to the Court for an increase
of wages. When work is plentiful and labour scarce,
the demand is ever made for higher pay.

In the Capital there is a Government labour department which has been in existence for 19 years.
It supervises the various labour regulations, and the
various agencies or labour bureaux throughout the
Dominion. The annual cost of the department is about
£27,000. This includes the cost of administering the
Industrial Conciliation and Arbitration Act. There
are labour offices or bureaux throughout New Zealand,
and in four of the cities there is a department
to look after the unemployed. These branches deal
with the unemployed, finding work for them and
aiding them to get work. In the year ending 31st
March, 1909, 10,391 were so helped, 4,190 being placed
with private employers and 6,201 on Government
works. Those placed in Government works were
mostly labourers, being 5,901 out of the 6,201 employed. The Government has always a considerable
number of public works in progress, railways, roads,
tracks, coal mines, etc., and the number of labourers
employed by the State is therefore large. During

last year there was in the winter months a considerable number of unemployed, as there had been a
shrinkage in the price of wool, and of some of the
other staple products of the country.

There is, as exists in England, a Workers' Compensation Act. It varies in some of its provisions
from the English statute, but not in many vital
details.

Section III

LAND LEGISLATION

The first settlers who landed in New Zealand
bought land from the Maoris before the proclamation
in 1840 of the Queen's sovereignty. The land was
unsurveyed, and the settlers were not always careful
to investigate the title of those who conveyed it to
them. The price given was often most inadequate.
Thousands of acres were sold in exchange for goods
of small value. In 1840 a treaty was made with the
Maoris, being first signed near the mouth of the
Waitangi river in the Bay of Islands. This treaty,
as has been said, was called the Treaty of Waitangi,
and is to-day looked upon by the Maoris with more
reverence than Englishmen treat "Magna Charta"
or "The Bill of Rights." Its provisions have already

been set out in the chapter dealing with the early history of the Dominion.

At the time the treaty was made large tracts of land had been purchased by the New Zealand Company ; and how one large tract, upon part of which the city of Wellington now stands, was purchased is related by Mr E. J. Wakefield in his book *Adventure in New Zealand.* Mr Wakefield describes the meetings with the natives and the long discussions with the chiefs, without which no business could be done with the ancient Maoris. There were several meetings on succeeding days, during which the advantages and disadvantages likely to accrue to the natives were discussed by both parties, before the chiefs signified their assent to a sale and fixed the boundaries of the land to be alienated. He goes on to detail the circumstances in connection with the fixing of the price, the approval and acceptance by the chiefs of the goods offered and the final signing of the deed of conveyance. This is the story given in his own words :—

" This morning, the goods which Colonel Wakefield intended to give the natives for their land were got upon deck, in the presence of about a hundred of the natives. Except incessant chattering, they offered no obstruction or inconvenience to this process ; but as they filled up a good deal of room on deck, which was wanted in order to assort the various things, my uncle requested Wharepouri to explain this and get them to go ashore until all was ready. He instantly addressed them from the hurricane-house, and set the example of going on shore himself, which was readily and expeditiously followed by all. . . .

"When all the articles had been selected and arranged, a message was sent on shore for all the chiefs, who came accompanied by their sons. They examined the stock of goods strictly and carefully, and approved of the quality and quantity. . . .

"I had prepared a deed according to Colonel Wakefield's instructions, nearly in the words of some deeds which we had on board, that had been drawn on the model of those used by missionary land-buyers in the northern part of the island. The boundaries and native names being inserted from Wharepouri's dictation, the deed was brought on deck, and laid on the capstan. As I read it through, sentence by sentence, in English, Barrett interpreted into Maori ; and he was repeatedly urged by Colonel Wakefield to explain fully each important provision contained in it. The native reserves were especially dwelt upon. Although the natives had repeatedly discussed every point, and this was therefore only a repetition of the agreement to which they had all given an ample assent on several occasions, and though they were anxious to get the goods on shore, and the distribution ended, they listened with great attention and decorum to the recapitulation of the deed in both languages. The chiefs then came up in succession to the capstan in order to make their marks. As each one's name was called I wrote it down, and held the pen whilst he made a mark opposite. They all brought their sons with them, in order, as they suggested, to bind them in the transaction and to prove that they looked forward to the future.

"The boats were then sent away with the goods to the settlements, the chief of each accompanying them, and undertaking to distribute them at his own place."

In 1839, although the sovereignty had not then been proclaimed, the Secretary of State for the Colonies had declared that the Government would not recognise any titles to land in New Zealand which were not afterwards confirmed by the Government. The Governor and Legislative Council of New South Wales proceeded, in 1840, to act according to the instruction of the Secretary of State, and passed an Act empowering the Government to appoint commissioners to examine and report on land claims in New Zealand. The second ordinance passed by the Governor and Legislative Council of New Zealand (9th June, 1841) repealed the Act of New South Wales, and determined the commission. The ordinance repeated the declaration in the New South Wales Act that no titles to land were valid unless

recognised by the Queen, and authorised the Governor
to appoint a commission to examine and report on
all claims to land. It declared that the commissioners
were to be guided by the real justice and good conscience of the case. A certain value appearing in
schedule "B" of the ordinance was to be deemed the
fair value of the land. The rate varied from 6d. per
acre in 1815–24 to from 4s. to 8s. in 1839. There
were other conditions set forth in the ordinance. The
work begun by this commission was continued by
other commissioners and land claims judges till 1878,
and even since then the Government has recognised
some claims. There were various amendments made
in this ordinance, and one amendment was to restrict
the area that would be recognised as acquired. As a
complement to this ordinance it was declared by an
ordinance in 1842 that all lands validly sold by the
Maoris were vested in Her Majesty as part of the
demesne of the Crown. This was necessary to give a
good title to the persons found to be purchasers.

After the Treaty of Waitangi, the Government had
to acquire land for settlement from the Maoris by
purchase, and purchases began shortly after the year
1841. No land has ever been taken from the Maoris
save by purchase except in the case of land confiscated in some districts because of the rebellion of
the Maori owners. It was not till 1849 that a Crown
Lands Ordinance was passed. Prior to this date the

settlers in the various parts of the country had obtained their land from the New Zealand Company, or from the associations that had founded the different settlements. It is unnecessary to detail the diverse and varied schemes adopted to dispose of Crown lands. The schemes varied with the district. In Canterbury, save when the Governor issued regulations reducing for a time the price of land, land was sold on a system of free selection before survey at a uniform rate of £2 per acre, a system that continued down to 1877. This was what was called the Wakefield system. In Otago there were many methods adopted of disposing of lands, by auction, by selection after survey, on deferred payments, and many others. In the North Island land was less readily acquired, as the natives were numerous, and purchases from natives were often slow in completion, and as in many districts the land was covered with forest, roads were few and badly made. Different systems of land disposal have continued down to the present day. The usual method is to open a block for settlement and to give the land, if there is competition, to the person who obtains it by ballot, provided he has enough capital to work it and has no other land. The area one can acquire is limited, and if the purchaser is the proprietor of a certain area he cannot obtain land from the Crown. There is now a leasing system without the right of purchase, with provision for renewal of leases and for permanent improvements remaining the property of the lessee.

Various restrictions exist to prevent land monopoly, and to secure occupation and utilisation of the lands. In 1892 a system was originated of the compulsory acquisition of land for small or closer settlement. This still exists, and what may be done now to secure private lands may be briefly stated. The land to be acquired must be suitable for (a) settlement, or (b) providing land for sites for homesteads on pastoral Crown lands, or (c) providing low-lying land necessary for working neighbouring pastoral Crown land, or (d) exchanging high land only suitable for pastoral purposes for low-lying land suitable for agriculture, or (e) providing land by purchase or exchange to consolidate any estate or to adjust its boundaries. It is almost entirely under (a) that estates have been acquired. In some instances the owners have made agreements with the Government, but in most there has been compulsory acquisition. The minimum area that can be acquired compulsorily is, in the case of country land, any amount over 1000 acres of first-class land, 2000 acres of second-class land, or 5000 acres of third-class land. Of land within five miles of a city any area over 200 acres may be taken. Land may also be taken for workers' homes in a borough if the population is 15,000 or over. The

mode of taking is to gazette the requisition and serve
a copy of it on the owner. The owner must then,
within 42 days, make his claim. He may object to
the taking, and if so, his objection must be heard by
a Court consisting of a Supreme Court Judge and
two assessors, one appointed by the claimant and one
by the Minister of Lands. The owner also states the
monetary amount of his claim. There are various
matters dealt with in such claims. After the land is
classified by the Court, the Court determines what
land may be taken and the compensation to be paid.
The compensation can only be (1) the value of the
land, and (2) the loss to the claimant's business by
taking the land. All land is valued at its unimproved
value in New Zealand and entered on an assessment
roll. The improvements have to be ascertained by
evidence. There is a percentage added to the unimproved value of 10 per cent. if the land value is under
£50,000, and if it exceeds £50,000, then 10 per cent.
for the £50,000 and 5 per cent. for the sum in excess
of £50,000. The owner can, on the assessment roll,
always fix his own value, but on that value he has to
pay his land tax.

The land so acquired is disposed of on perpetual
renewable leases of 33 years at a rental of £4. 10s.
per cent. on the amount paid for the land. At the
end of such lease the renewal rental is £4. 10s. per
cent. on the value of the land. If there are more

eligible applicants than one, then the ballot settles who is entitled to the lease. These are the main provisions for obtaining private land for settlement and for its disposal when acquired.

During recent years the system of leasing has been attacked, and there is a strong party, especially amongst the Crown tenants, who are anxious to obtain the freehold, and to have the option of purchase, contrary to the provisions of the leases granted to them.

The area of private freehold land acquired under the compulsory system was, up to March, 1910, 1,238,097 acres. The rentals from the leased lands exceed the interest on the sums borrowed to acquire the estates. Under this system 4416 settlers have been placed upon the land by the Government.

CHAPTER VI

THE OUTLOOK

WHAT is to be the future of New Zealand and her people? The climate is one of the finest in the world for health and enjoyment. The health of the people is far above the average of other countries. The robust stock of its fathers has not, so far, been debilitated by even the sunny warmth of the far north. The race to come should be physically strong and mentally keen.

The British respect for law has been handed down to the native born, and this, with the freedom from debasing poverty, will help to uplift their social life and to keep it on a higher plane. Although generous, they are not without thrift. Their accumulated wealth is great. With a healthy climate, with strength and thrift and an ingrained respect for law and order, why should not the race, surrounded by the lavish gifts of nature, become a noble one?

New Zealanders, it may be, are more readily influenced by new ideas of social duty than those who live under the domination of ancient institutions and in lands crowded with historical associations. Free and untrammelled, they hear the primitive call of brotherhood, learnt in the pioneer fight shoulder to shoulder in a new land. The parent-land is the gainer, and she has not yet forgotten the splendid response to the call to arms in the South African war, or the voluntary support of her first line of defence. This same sentiment is apparent in the social legislation of the New Zealanders. The great organisation of the State is being used to give an equal chance to all. They may fail, and their experiments may show that the ever-present danger of a true democracy lies in the deadening of individual energy and enterprise by the growth of an all-embracing State interference. But if they fail, their strivings will not have been in vain, though humanity be the poorer for their failure. For the present, they feel that State control is better than to be the slaves of monopolising companies or autocratic millionaires, or to be strangled in the grip of all-powerful trusts. So long as there is individual liberty, free speech and a free life, they think that monopolies, which seem ever-present in civilised societies, should be controlled by persons under their authority rather than by those who can dictate to them.

Already there are many favourable portents. Literature of the soil is being produced. Poets kindled with the fire of genius have arisen. In music and in art the native-born talent is forcing recognition. The second and third generations of New Zealanders are now coming to the front, men and women who have not seen the old lands, and whose knowledge of the greater world has been culled from books. These true New Zealanders, when the opportunity offers to go abroad and compete with the world's best in the universities, in the musical colleges and art schools, and in commerce, hold their own. They are alert and intelligent. Optimistic and cheerful, they are armed with the sword of hope and the shield of faith. Trials will no doubt obstruct them and evils baulk them, but if they fail many others will be routed. No, we who have lived long in New Zealand have hope in her, and in her people, and believe that when the books are closed, and her history written, there will be said of her, "Well done!"

> "These things shall be: a loftier race
>   Than e'er the world has known shall rise,
> With flame of freedom in their souls
>   And light of knowledge in their eyes."

INDEX

www.ingramcontent.com/pod-product-compliance
Ingram Content Group UK Ltd.
Pitfield, Milton Keynes, MK11 3LW, UK
UKHW042143280225
455719UK00001B/68

9 781107 630406